Images of Life on Children's Television

Action for Children's Television (ACT) is a national nonprofit organization that works to improve children's experiences with television through legal advocacy, parent and teacher education, and dialogue with broadcasters and cablecasters.

Founded in 1968, ACT's primary goal is to increase the diversity of programming available to young audiences. ACT has twenty thousand national members and the support of more than 150 major organizations concerned with children.

IMAGES OF LIFE ON CHILDREN'S TELEVISION

Sex Roles, Minorities, and Families

F. Earle Barcus, Ph.D.

Action for Children's Television (ACT)

PRAEGER

PRAEGER SPECIAL STUDIES • PRAEGER SCIENTIFIC

Library of Congress Cataloging in Publication Data

Barcus, Francis Earle, 1927-
   Images of life on children's television.

   Includes bibliographies and indexes.
   1. Television and children—United States.
2. Sex role—United States.   3. Minorities in
television—United States.   4. Television and
family—United States.   I. Title.
HQ784.T4B356   1983   305.2'3   83-4131
ISBN 0-03-063883-6

Published in 1983 by Praeger Publishers
CBS Educational and Professional Publishing
a Division of CBS Inc.
521 Fifth Avenue, New York, NY 10175 USA
© Praeger Publishers

 456789 052 98765432

Printed in the United States of America
on acid-free paper

Action for Children's Television is grateful for the support of Carnegie Corporation of New York and The Ford Foundation, which made this book possible.

Acknowledgments

Judith Schaefer, who worked with me throughout these studies as chief research supervisor, is primarily responsible for the background research that reviews the substantial and expanding literature on sex-role development and television portrayals. I feel indeed fortunate to have had her working with me. Through her diligent and devoted efforts, this book is more thorough and accurate than it otherwise might have been.

Special thanks are also due to Bernadette Nelson for her editorial suggestions on the chapter reviewing the literature on minorities and television.

Appreciation is also due to the three coders who worked throughout the hot summer months, paying great attention to detail in the content analysis: Kim Devolve, Christina Cruz, and Edward Hazell. In addition, Carol Schaffer acted in a most professional and efficient manner as computer consultant for data analysis and statistical work.

Finally, I would like to thank Action for Children's Television for its support of these studies and its patience in seeing them completed.

F. Earle Barcus

Contents

Tables

Introduction

In the United States, children between 2 and 11 years of age spend an average of about four hours per day watching television. Some children watch much less. To make up the average, for every child who watches one hour per day, there must be another who watches seven hours; for every child who watches two hours, another is watching six hours. Thus, from a very young age, television is an important part of the child's learning environment.

Although it is true that children watch adult television as well as programs designed for and directed to children, it is precisely because there are programs directed at the child audience that they deserve special analysis. The amount of time the child watches television is a prime responsibility of parents. What there is for the child to watch, however, is the responsibility of the people in the television industry: the writers, directors, and producers who make programs; the companies and advertisers who pay for them; and the networks, cable companies, syndicators, and stations that distribute them. It is important to remember that children's television scheduling is intentional—the content of the programs the television industry provides for children is specifically chosen with young audiences in mind.

The rationale for this book is based on the knowledge that children learn from their environment. They learn social roles and behaviors through observing, imitating, and modeling themselves on parents, siblings, peers, teachers, and important others around them. But it is also true that an important part of the child's environment is television. Children learn values, social roles, and behaviors through observation of the characters, situations, conflicts, and other aspects of the portrayals of life on television.

The data reported in this book are a result of studies conducted by using a sample of nearly 50 hours of network and independent-station programs for the child audience during one week in January 1981. The studies were conducted in four parts: investigation of the programs as a whole; study of sex-role behaviors of the characters in the programs; study of minority-character portrayals; and study of family and kinship relations depicted.

Part I describes the theoretical approach and the procedures used for the study of life representations in cartoons and other children's programs. The fundamental unit of analysis is the program segment (drama, cartoon, comedy, or informational segment). These segments are discreet slices of life with a focus on certain topics, taking place in various settings, and populated by a variety of characters in different sexual, ethnic, familial, occupational, and other roles. The analysis of these program segments in Part I thus represents the context and defines the parameters of the world of children's television.

Part II focuses on how the sexes are portrayed in this world. Here, we have based the analysis on the use of the concepts of "recognition" and "respect" as a model to evaluate the portrayals of female and male characters. "Recognition" refers to the frequencies with which certain characters appear. "Respect" means the treatment of the characters in the programs.*

The portrayal of the sexes is a particularly important subject for study because of changing roles of men and women today. As a learning environment for children, children's television is especially important. One major question is how (or whether) children's television is reflecting these changes. Another relates to what children's television is teaching children about their own sex-role identities, sex-role expectations of others, and behaviors to imitate.

In Part III the focus is on the portrayals of minority and ethnic groups. It deals not only with the traditional U.S. minorities, such as blacks and Hispanics (who have been the focus of much of the research to date), but also with people (Americans or foreigners) of identifiable national origins—English, Irish, German, Chinese, Japanese, Eskimo, and others. The model of recognition and respect is applied here as well.

Past research has revealed that for many children, television is their only source of information about minorities and people of diverse nationalities and ethnic backgrounds. These portrayals are important both for majority children, who are learning about people who are different from them, and for minority children, who are viewing role models of their own ethnic backgrounds. What does children's television teach these children?

Finally, in Part IV, the focus is on the family and other kinship portrayals. The portrayal of families on television is a particularly important subject for study today because of changes taking place in the role of the family in society. In many ways, traditional family functions of education, socialization, security, and support have been at least partially taken over by other social institutions. At the same time, these traditional family functions are being reexamined as important factors in the stability of the social structure and in the rearing of the child.

One major question on which we try to provide some insight here is the extent to which television is reflecting traditional and changing patterns of family life. What is children's television teaching children about the world beyond their own homes and families and about how other

---

*These concepts are adapted from Clark's (1969) article dealing with the stages of minority-group acceptance into the media and the relationship to social control.

family units live and behave? Are these television families providing learning models the child may use in parent-child relations and conflict situations within the family?

Parts II, III, and IV of the book each include a summary of the research literature relevant to its particular topic: sex roles, minorities, or family life. The substantial bibliographies at the end of the book provide the interested reader with further sources of information in these three areas.

Images of Life on Children's Television

I
Representations of Life on Children's Television

1 THE STUDY OF LIFE REPRESENTATIONS

What are some of the things children view on children's TV programs? What kinds of content are available for imitation and observational learning?

First, all media presentations, including children's television, are selective in the kinds of stories that are presented to the audience. Writers, producers, directors, and others select the sequence of events we call the plot. They select types of characters—by sex, age, race, social status, occupation, marital status, etc.—to fill the roles and tell the stories. They are responsible also for the manner in which these stories are told—by a comedy or through adventure; by animation or real-life presentation; film or video; and long or short programs. And they devise the ways that conflicts are resolved and decide which social values are upheld.

Whether these selections are intentional or unintentional, the results of this selective process can be seen in the programs—often with surprising consistency. Thus if, as was found in these studies, 78 percent of the 1,107 characters indentified by sex are male, there is an implicit message for the child viewer: that males are more often recognized, more visible, and more important than females.

The frequencies with which sexes, age groups, and racial and ethnic minorities are portrayed are thus measures of the recognition given to these groups.

Second, writers, producers, and others are not only responsible for the frequencies with which characters and groups are selected for portrayal, but also for their assignment to various roles. Thus, characters may be placed in exciting contexts or humorous ones; they can be heroes, villains, or relegated to minor roles; and they can occupy high- or low-status occupations.

In the selection and presentation of roles are further implicit messages for child viewers. They may learn who is important, who leads the most exciting lives, and who are the winners and who are the losers.

The distributions and assignment of roles provide measures of respect for individuals and groups.

Third, aspects of TV that provide lessons for the child viewer are those value orientations of characters in TV programs. In the child's socialization process, he or she is taught, by parents, teachers, the church, friends, and television, which things in life are to be sought after, and which are valued most by those with whom he or she identifies. He or she may not only learn lessons of morality and the importance of love, friendship, justice, respect, and loyalty, but also practical lessons about the importance of work, knowledge, wealth, power, and hatred. These may be learned explicitly by observing the aims and goals of characters or implicitly through the selection and assignment of roles.

In short, children's television programs provide a value orientation or an expression of what is right and what is wrong.

Another important component of children's television programs is the behaviors of the characters. Although TV characters behave in many different ways, there are some which may be selected as salient for the child viewer. For example, in attempting to achieve the desired aims and goals referred to above, how do characters behave? That is, what means are used; what barriers are faced?

In past research, many studies have focused on interpersonal physical violence as an important behavioral means of problem solving in children's television. The results of these studies led the surgeon general of the United States to state that evidence of a relationship between viewing violence on television and the stimulation of aggression in children was sufficient to take action to reduce the amount of violence on television—especially that viewed by children.

In this research, violence is looked at as simply one of several behaviors by which television characters attempt to attain goals and solve problems. Albeit an important one, violent behavior is only one among a number of choices TV characters select from to solve problems. There are many other choices in life, as well as in TV. Examples are substituting persuasion for violence, using legal authority (e.g., calling police), using one's personal charm, utilizing trickery or deceit, or simply applying hard work, diligence, and intelligent planning. These studies focus on all of these behaviors that may be learned by the child viewer.

Other behaviors analyzed in these studies relate to sex-role behaviors of males and females portrayed in the stories. If, as past research has demonstrated, children use television characters as models for imitation and develop expectations of how significant others behave, then a study of such behavior should reveal patterns and examples from which the child viewer may choose. In these studies, such behaviors as aggression, activity, curiosity, and impulsivity, as well as evidence of anxiety, the importance of social relationships, self-concept, and achievement-related behaviors, are the focus of analysis dealing with sex-role patterns.

Finally, imitative and modeling effects may be assumed to occur as the child observes various personality and physical traits evidenced by the characters. To study this aspect of TV's portrayal of life, the major characters in the stories have been rated, by using several semantic-differential-type scales dealing with characters' strength, goodness, kindness, intelligence, honesty, warmth, and activity, as well as with whether they are shown as independent or dependent, peaceful or violent, active or passive, and serious or humorous. Personal appearance, dress, and agility are other factors considered.

Other important areas for study that are not addressed here are the interaction patterns and interrelationships between and among characters in the stories. These patterns are looked at to some extent in the analysis of family relationships included as part of this series, and have been the focus of some previously conducted research (Greenberg, 1980).

In summary, there are five aspects of life discussed above that are seen as important and relevant content for child learning and imitation: recognition of certain people and groups; respect given in role assignments; value orientations illustrated through the major aims and goals of various roles; behavioral patterns, especially with regard to means of achieving goals and solving problems; and personality traits evidenced by characters.

2 PROCEDURES

The data for this study were derived from a sample of available commercial children's TV programs broadcast in Boston in January 1981 (a procedural appendix is included as Appendix A). The sample selected and recorded for analysis included all programming intended for or addressed to children on Saturday and Sunday on six commercial stations, plus one weekday of morning and afternoon programming for each station.* The resulting sample is given in Table 2.1 (see Appendix B for a detailed program list).

RECORDING PROCEDURES

All programs were recorded on one-half-inch videotape and simultaneously monitored and timed by a digital readout clock for all program and nonprogram elements. These included program matter, opening and closing credits, commercial announcements, noncommercial public service announcements, program promotional announcements, transitional material (e.g., "We'll be right back after these messages"), and other miscellaneous items, such as station ID announcements and dead air. Each of these elements was timed to the nearest five seconds and written on screening sheets developed to record half an hour of program time each.

Each program segment (cartoon, story, news program, etc.) was then identified and serial-identification numbers and length of the segment were assigned.

---

*Two stations (WBZ and WCVB) aired no weekday children's programs during the sample week.

Table 2.1   Sample of Children's Programs Studied

STATION	DAY	FROM–TO	TOTAL TIME (HOURS: MINUTES)
WBZ, Ch. 4 (NBC)	Sat., 1/10/81	6:30a–1:30p*	7:00
	Sun., 1/18/81	7:30a–9:00a	1:30
WCVB, Ch. 5 (ABC)	Sat., 1/10/81	6:30a–12:00n	5:30
	Sun., 1/18/81	7:00a–9:00a	2:00
WNAC, Ch. 7 (CBS)	Sat., 1/10/81	8:00a–2:00p	6:00
	Tue., 1/13/81	8:00a–9:00a	1:00
WXNE, Ch. 25 (ind.)	Sat., 1/17/81	7:00a–8:00a	1:00
		8:30a–9:00a	:30
	Tue., 1/13/81	6:30a–10:00a	3:30
		2:00p–4:00p	2:00
WSBK, Ch. 38 (ind.)	Sat., 1/17/81	8:30a–10:00a	1:30
	Sun., 1/11/81	7:00a–10:30a	3:30
	Tue., 1/13/81	6:30a–9:00a	2:30
WLVI, Ch. 56 (ind.)	Sun., 1/11/81	7:30a–12:00n	4:30
	Tue., 1/13/81	1:00p–5:00p	4:00
	Fri., 1/16/81	7:00a–10:00a	3:00
Total			49:00

*A.M. is indicated by "a" and P.M. by "p."

Coding categories and forms were developed for each basic unit of analysis pertinent to the studies: program segments, characters, and family-kinship units.

Category Development and Coding Reliability

After preliminary categories for program segments, characters, and family units were developed, three coders were instructed in their use. Then each coder independently coded a sample of 30 program segments for program and character data. The objective was to obtain a minimum of 80 percent reliability of agreement among coders. After the first reliability test, those categories or category sets that did not equal or exceed the minimum reliability level were discussed, altered, further defined, or dropped from the analysis. Another reliability check was then conducted. In the final check all category sets met the minimum reliability standards or better.

In addition, the forms were later edited for consistency and completeness of coding. An additional precaution was taken to insure coding accuracy: Each coder was required to write, in the "notes" section of each coding form, an explanation of several of the more difficult codes—for example, specific occupations, explanations of sex-role behaviors, and goals of the characters. This allowed for later checking of the reasoning behind the simple code-number decisions.

Coders then played and replayed tapes of each program segment, classifying for program and character information. The family analysis was conducted at a later date after family units were identified in some of the program segments.

Resultant Data and Analysis

The above procedures yielded a total of 235 program-segment coding forms, 1,145 character forms, and 114 family-kinship forms. Each set of forms was then keypunched and processed at the Boston University Computing Center.

Computer analysis utilized the Statistical Package for the Social Science (SPSS) program. In addition to calculating frequencies and percentages for the various cross-breaks in the report, statistical tests of significance were run by utilizing the chi-square, t-tests, and the Mann-Whitney "U" test when groups were small and t-test assumptions could not be made.

In this study, approximately 38 out of the 49 hours recorded were classified as program time included in the program segments. This is about 78 percent of total time. The segments ranged from short, one-minute "drop-ins" to one of 50 minutes ("Captain Kangaroo"). The average length of all segments was 9.7 minutes, with the most frequent length being six minutes. Seventy-one percent of all segments were ten minutes or less.

Table 2.2 shows the number of segments and minutes of program-segment time, by station, origin, and day of the week. Approximately 45 percent of the segments (35 percent of the time) were current network programs, and approximately three-fourths were broadcast on Saturday and Sunday mornings. Only nine of the 235 segments (4 percent) originated locally.

Table 2.2   Distribution of Program Segments

DISTRIBUTION VARIABLE	NUMBER OF SEGMENTS	PERCENT	MINUTES	PERCENT
By channel				
4 (NBC)	48	20.4	412	18.0
5 (ABC)	39	16.6	350	15.3
7 (CBS)	42	17.9	328	14.4
25 (ind.)	16	6.8	298	13.0
38 (ind.)	27	11.5	356	15.6
56 (ind.)	63	26.8	542	23.7
By day				
Saturday	121	51.5	1,016	44.5
Sunday	52	22.1	545	23.8
Weekday	62	26.4	725	31.7

Table 2.2   Distribution of Program Segments (cont.)

DISTRIBUTION VARIABLE	NUMBER OF SEGMENTS	PERCENT	MINUTES	PERCENT
By origin				
Network	106	45.1	799	34.9
Local	9	3.8	102	4.5
Recorded/syndicated	120	51.1	1,385	60.6
Total	235	100.0	2,286	100.0

3 PROGRAM CONTEXTS: DESCRIBING THE WORLD OF COMMERCIAL CHILDREN'S TELEVISION

Since all character and family data were drawn from the basic sample of 235 program segments, these provide the context in which the characters operate. The program types and settings; the major subjects dealt with in the plots; the extent to which programs deal with family relations, ethnicity, the elderly, and the handicapped; and the racial and sexual distributions of characters in the programs—all these describe the world in which characters live.

TYPES OF PROGRAMS AND THE USE OF ANIMATION

The world of commercial children's TV is primarily an animated one. Three-fourths of the 235 segments studied were animated cartoons.* These accounted for two-thirds of the total time, or 25 of the 38 hours studied.

Overall, 71 percent of all program segments (accounting for almost 77 percent of total time) were devoted to entertainment programs. These were primarily cartoon comedies and action/adventure dramas (see Table 3.1). These two program types accounted for 62 percent of all segments studied (61 percent of total time), and 87 percent of all entertainment-type programming (80 percent of entertainment-program time). By definition, all of the cartoon comedies were animated

---

*These include not only the traditional "Bugs Bunny" or "Popeye" cartoon comedies, but also animated action/adventure shows, such as "Spiderwoman," "Batman," or "Thundarr the Barbarian," as well as animated versions of family or situation comedies, such as the "Partridge Family" or "Gilligan's Island."

Table 3.1   Types of Programs and Use of Animation

PROGRAM TYPE[a]	NO. OF SEGMENTS	PERCENT	MINUTES OF TIME	PERCENT	PERCENT ANIMATED[b]
Cartoon comedy	114	48.5	846	37.0	100.0
Other comedy drama	5	2.1	97	4.2	27.8
Action/adventure drama	31	13.2	547	23.9	91.4
Other drama	13	5.5	183	8.0	50.8
Other entertainment	4	1.7	73	3.2	0.0
Informational programs	68	29.0	540	23.6	7.4
Total	235	100.0	2286	100.0	65.9

[a]Examples of program types: cartoon comedy: "Tom and Jerry," "Bugs Bunny," "Underdog," "Scoobydo," "Flintstones"; other comedy drama: "Partridge Family," "Brady Bunch," "Leave It to Beaver"; action adventure: includes Westerns ("Lone Ranger"), fantasy/science fiction ("Force Five," "Thundarr"), crime ("Batman," "Spiderwoman"), action ("Mighty Mouse," "Johnny Quest"); other drama: "Fat Albert," "Davey and Goliath," "Barbapapa"; other entertainment: "Bozo's Big Top," "Great Space Coaster," "Willie Whistle"; informational: includes children's news ("Ask NBC News," "In the News"), drop-ins ("Snipets," "Schoolhouse Rock," "Time Out"), interviews ("For Kids Only," "Get Off Your Block"), foreign language ("Villa Allegre"), and others ("Jabberwocky," "Hot Fudge").

[b]Percent of the minutes of time in each category that was animated programming.

programming. Moreover, 94 percent of all action/adventure programming was animated.† Informational programming accounted for 29 percent of all segments, representing about 24 percent of total time. Few informational programs were animated.

Settings

More than 70 percent of segments that could be identified as to setting took place in the United States and 10 percent occurred in foreign lands. The most frequent setting within these locations was in the city or suburban environment (46 percent), and rural settings (32 percent) and other or unknown settings constituting the remainder (see Table 3.2).

Most segments were also set in current or contemporary time periods (72 percent), with less emphasis on historical periods (15 percent of segments) or on the future (4 percent).

†The only nonanimated action/adventure segments were reruns of "Batman" and "Superman" on one independent UHF station. All of the current network adventure programs were animated.

Table 3.2 Settings of the Programs

SETTING	NUMBER OF SEGMENTS	PERCENT
Urban-rural		
City, suburban	107	45.5
Rural, country	74	31.5
Other (at sea, etc.)	13	5.5
Unknown	45	17.5
U.S.-foreign		
United States	130	55.3
Foreign country	17	7.3
Other (at sea, etc.)	16	6.8
Studio settings	16	6.8
Unknown	56	23.8
Time		
Distant past	36	15.3
Recent past	5	2.1
Current-contemporary	169	71.9
Future	10	4.3
Uncertain	15	6.4
Total	235	100.0

Subject Matter

Subject matter of the programs illustrates the concerns of the world of children's television. What were the programs about? When classified by major and minor subjects, six major categories seemed to predominate (see Table 3.3). Interpersonal rivalry between characters, represented by relatively plotless cartoons such as "Bugs Bunny" or "Road Runner," was most frequent in the segments, followed by the subjects of crime, domestic relations, nature, the entertainment world, and science. These six categories accounted for 62 percent of all subject-matter classifications. Infrequently dealt with, accounting for 3 percent or less of the combined major or minor subject matter, were the categories of religion, language, the armed forces and war, education, love and romance, the business world, historical topics, race and nationality, the fine arts, crafts, health, and social relations. In children's television, the focus of attention is indeed quite limited.

Program Relevancies

Relevancies refer to the extent to which certain aspects of life are dealt with in any way in children's television programs. Four were de-

Table 3.3 Subject Areas Dealt with in the Programs

SUBJECT-MATTER CATEGORY	MAJOR SUBJECT	MINOR SUBJECT	COMBINED[a]
Interpersonal rivalry (conflicts, jealousies, fighting between characters)	22%	11%	19%
Crime (thieves, police, crime detection)	16	1	11
Domestic (marriage, home, family affairs)	5	18	10
Nature and animals (hunting, exploring, etc.)	7	8	8
Entertainment world (sports, show business)	4	14	7
Science (scientists, technology, space exploration)	6	10	7
Supernatural (magic, the occult)	4	4	4
Government/public affairs (law, politics)	4	2	3
Race/nationality	1	7	3
Literature/arts	3	3	3
Historical (association with historical events)	2	5	3
Crafts/hobbies	2	3	3
Health/nutrition/physical fitness	3	2	3
Business and industry	3	2	3
Love and romance (relations between sexes)	2	3	2
Education (schools, teachers, training)	3	2	2
Personal and social relations (friendship, honesty, etc.)	3	1	2
Armed forces/war	2	—	1
Language (words, spelling, foreign languages)	1	2	1
Religion (church, clergy, religious customs)	—	1	—[b]
Other, miscellaneous	7	1	5
Total (percent)	100	100	100
Total (number of segments classified)	(235)	(117)	(352)

[a]Based on 352 classifications; some segments not classified for minor subject.

[b]Less than ½ of 1 percent.

fined and coded here: family relevance, defined as any reference to or portrayal of any type of family or kinship unit; ethnic relevance—a portrayal of or reference to any ethnic or racial group, even if only a minor character is represented; relevance to the elderly—segment topics or characters decline with older people; and relevance to the handicapped —as subject matter or character portrayals. The results are given in Table 3.4.

Four out of ten segments were in some way relevant for further study of family and kinship relations, slightly more relevant to ethnicity, and only 16 percent portrayed or referred to the aged. The handicapped are virtually invisible in the sample, with only three of 235 segments in any way referring to or portraying the handicapped.

When looking at program relevancies to family and ethnic relations, one can see that in many instances, the relevancy is based on the appearance of a character, or possibly on the setting of the story. Comparing relevancy with subject matter, for example, domestic or family relationships accounted for only 10 percent of all subject-matter classifications, although 40 percent of the segments may have had some relevancy through portrayals of kinship relations such as brother-and-sister characters in the story. Similarly, although ethnic relations were coded for nearly 45 percent of the segments, a similar subject category of race/nationality appears as a major subject category in only 1 percent of the segments, and as a minor subject in only 7 percent.

Character Distributions

Program segments were also classified in terms of their character composition (see Table 3.5).

In terms of racial composition, only 18 percent of the segments represented integrated worlds where both white and black or other minority characters appeared together. In contrast, 56 percent contained only white characters (or white with animal characters), whereas only 2 percent had only black. In the remainder there were no human characters, and these were not classified as to racial composition.

Table 3.4 Program Relevancies

RELEVANCY	NUMBER OF SEGMENTS	PERCENT OF 235 PROGRAM SEGMENTS
Family relations	94	40.0
Ethnic relations	105	44.7
The elderly	37	15.7
The handicapped	3	1.3

Table 3.5 Distribution of Characters in the Programs, by Race and Sex

DISTRIBUTION	NUMBER OF SEGMENTS	PERCENT
By racial identification		
White characters only	131	55.7
Black characters only	4	1.7
Mixed white, black, other	42	17.9
Other minorities only	2	0.9
No human characters	56	23.8
	235	100.0
By sex of character		
Male characters only	82	34.9
Female characters only	4	1.7
Mixed male and female	132	56.2
Other	·2	0.8
No characters in program	15	6.4
Total	235	100.0

Distribution of the sexes illustrates a male dominance in children's TV. Although 56 percent of the segments were sexually integrated, with males and females appearing together, 35 percent contained only male characters, whereas a mere 2 percent had only female.

In sum, the program-segment information provides us with a kind of snapshot of the world of children's television. This world is predominantly populated by animated characters involved in comedy and adventure. The action takes place in contemporary settings, primarily in the United States and in both city and rural areas.

Prime concerns are with personal rivalries, crime, and domestic affairs; nature and animals, the entertainment world, and science and technology receive some attention. There is much less concern for religion, war, education, love and romance, and other aspects of public and private life.

The world of children's TV is not well integrated racially. White characters most often appear without the company of blacks or other minorities, and animals are plentiful.

Males are important figures in children's TV, and often join together in single-sex groups to have fun, fight, or solve problems. This pattern of single-sex companionship is denied females, who seldom appear without the company of men.

There is also no great concern for the elderly, who appeared in only three out of 20 segments, and the handicapped barely exist in this world. A closer inspection of the population of this world—their numbers, role importance, goals, behaviors, and traits—is made in the chapters that follow.

II
Sex Roles and Behaviors

4 TV PORTRAYALS AND SEX-ROLE DEVELOPMENT

Television provides children with a powerful set of standards for behaviors. The child audience is uniquely vulnerable to televised presentations, particularly those in programming directed at children. What young people see on TV can lead to the learning and performance of similar social behaviors. The role television plays in the development of a child has been one of the most extensively examined areas of mass-communication research (Culley, Lazer, and Atkin, 1976, p. 3). Although the effects of specific media content on the child viewer are complex, recent research has provided evidence of a causal relationship between children's perceptions and exposure to TV programs.

Several studies have shown that television can teach different kinds of social behavior (Bandura, Ross, and Ross, 1963; Greenberg and Gordon, 1972; Stein and Friedrich, 1972). Children admit that they learn social behavior in viewing television (Schramm et al., 1961). When first graders were asked if they ever copied what they saw on television, more than 60 percent answered that they did, during a study conducted by Lyle and Hoffman (1972b).

In addition, younger viewers seem to be affected to a greater extent by television content, as noted by Collins (1975, pp. 35–36):

> . . . older children appear less affected than younger ones because they comprehend the complexities of television dramatic plots more effectively and, therefore, are more selectively affected by television portrayals. The idea becomes clearer when you consider the content of typical television entertainment programs. They include not only models of attitudes and social behavior, but also information about the appropriateness of those attitudes and actions, the motives behind them, and their consequences to the perpetrator and to others.

Preschool children are thought to be especially susceptible because they are less able than older children to separate fantasy from reality or to maintain some distance from their immediate perceptual experience (Stein and Friedrich, 1972, p. 205).

Although generally considered an entertainment source, television can teach a child to imitate values and behaviors contained in the programs. Television is an important component of the world seen through a child's eyes.

ROLE MODELS AND SEX-DIFFERENTIATED BEHAVIORS

Observational learning is a basic means by which people acquire and modify their behavior (Bandura, 1969). Mischel (1966), Kagan (1964) and Mussen et al. (1969), among many other social scientists, have investigated the learning of behavior through the observation of male and female role models.

Mischel determined that the very first step in acquiring sex-typed behaviors results from learning by the observation of live role models supplied by film, television, and books. These sex-role representations orient developing girls and boys as they shape their personalities, define values, and make decisions about the paths their lives will take. Mischel suggested that modeling effects are more probable when the observers have relatively little information about the appropriateness of a given behavior; thus children are made most vulnerable to this process.

Kagan (1964) has defined the sex-role standard, which he summarizes as the acquisition of knowledge regarding sex-appropriate behaviors and attributes, and their integration into the individual's self-concept in the forms of beliefs, attitudes, and behaviors. Kohlberg (1966) determined that sex-typed behavior develops from a set of organized rules that a child derives based on what he/she has seen and heard. Consequently, this sex-typing is affected by the child's perception of society's sex-role definitions and images.

As soon as they are born, children receive treatment from their parents that is responsive to the child's gender (Weitzman et al., 1970). Children find out that meaningful aspects of their lives have a great deal to do with masculinity and femininity. According to a "Nova" segment "The Pinks and the Blues," a program originally broadcast on PBS in September 1980:

> From the moment the newborn child is swaddled in a blue blanket, and his sister in a pink one, the two children are regarded differently. And thus begins the largely unconscious process of preparing boys to be men and girls to be women. Our preference for one sex over the other and the distinctions that we make from the very beginning set

in motion a pattern of treatment which continues right through childhood and probably life.

Role models supply individuals with information about appropriate
and socially acceptable sex-role behaviors. Nadelson (1974) and Yorburg
(1974) determined that a child's environment has a significant influence
on the development of sex-appropriate behaviors; Nadelson (reviewed in
Mayes and Valentine [1979]) described the entertainment elements in a
child's environment as a fantasy setting that gives the child an opportunity to "try on" a variety of roles.

Television programs for children have male and female characters
available as role models, and it has been documented by a number of
researchers that these characters teach children the appropriateness of
sex-role behaviors through the use of modeling. Since boys and girls are
exposed to the same models, however, imitation alone does not explain
why their sex-role behaviors are different. A variety of factors may have
a direct or an indirect effect upon the acquisition of sex-role behaviors
through observational learning.

Sex of the Model and the Viewer

Goff, Dysart, and Lehrer (1980) have investigated the relationship
between the sex role of the viewer and character perception. These researchers cited previous findings of Miller and Reeves (1976) concerning
the relationship between the viewer and identification with characters:

1. Young viewers identify with same-sex characters. This is almost uni-
   versal for boys, but not so for girls.
2. Boys identify with physical strength and activity levels.
3. Girls identify with physical attractiveness.

Research by Feldman, Vorwerk, and Rood (1977) showed that males
were more influenced by male-model performance than were females.
This pattern of greater same-sex model influence did not appear for females: "The present findings suggest that performance of models has a
differential effect upon observers, depending upon the sex of the
models, the success of the models, and the sex of the observer" (Feldman et al., 1977, p. 16).

The manner in which children imitate behaviors exhibited by same-
and opposite-sex models was also the focus of research by Perry and
Perry (1975). They classified elementary-school children as masculine or
feminine according to how they performed on a projective test of sex-
role behavior. Then the children were shown a film that portrayed the
behavior of an adult male and a female. Results of this experiment

showed that children of both sexes classified as masculine recalled more of the behavior of the male model, and that the "masculine" children also responded more spontaneously to the actions of the male model rather than those of the female model.

In reviewing the literature for their study of observational learning in children, Perry and Perry (1975 p. 1083) noted some work done by Grusec and Brinker (1972), which suggests that children generally learn more about like-sex models than opposite-sex models:

> These investigators discovered that elementary school boys learn more about the behavior of same-sex than of opposite-sex models (a similar, but less reliable result was found for girls). The authors argued that since children are ordinarily reinforced for imitating like-sex models, it becomes advantageous for them to learn as much as possible about what like-sex models do. In this way, they are in a better position to maximize the rewards they might later receive.

TRADITIONAL CONCEPTS OF MASCULINITY AND FEMININITY

Learning sex-differentiated behavior forms a person's psychological sex or gender role. Kagan (1964) contended that by the age of seven, young people are intensely committed to a sex-role identity that will not conflict with their perceptions about sex-appropriate behaviors. He also theorized that sex-role identity develops as the child matures intellectually, and that these changes parallel other aspects of cognitive growth. Sears et al. (1965) provided evidence that gender roles, once they are acquired, become highly resistant to change.

Each sex has an array of distinct roles and expectations assigned to it. Although some traits are shared by both sexes, many are considered appropriate to only one gender. The resulting categories of traits form the basis for sex-role stereotypes. The traditional division of male and female behaviors that has evolved in American culture is based on the concept of a dominant masculine stereotype and a more passive feminine stereotype. Forisha (1978, pp. 23–24) described it:

> According to the traditional stereotype, being masculine means being assertive, being interested in things rather than people, being analytical and manipulative, and being able to "get things done." Men are thought to be able to see themselves as separate from their environment. They are supposed to be able to stand back and analyze any problem—whether it has to do with people or things—and from this analysis be able to come up with a solution. Men are traditionally skilled in leadership. Violence is tolerated if men have to use it to defend their own rights or territory. According to this stereotype, men's sense of self-worth depends on meeting these expectations: being strong, analytical, and dominant.

According to the contrasting traditional stereotype for women, being feminine implies interdependence, interest in others, and a skill in interpersonal relationships. In all functions revolving around the biological and social spheres of life, women are supposed to be supreme. They are thought of as nurturing, tender, receptive, empathetic, and submissive. They smooth the way for others, namely men, who do not have such capabilities. The self-esteem of women is viewed as being derived from serving well and pleasing others, particularly men.

Hartley and Hardesty (1964) have demonstrated that boys are more firmly committed to, and are more aware of, the masculine stereotype at an earlier age than girls are correspondingly aware of the feminine stereotype. To assess the relative importance of various features of children's sex-role orientations, Katz (1979) designed a study that revealed that children begin elementary school with fairly stereotyped sex-role orientations that become more traditional as they grow older. Girls were found to be less flexible in personality traits and in views about who should perform traditionally feminine-stereotyped activities, and boys were found to be less flexible in occupational choices. Katz also determined that peer and media influences appear to be stronger correlates of sex-role flexibility in children than are perceived parental influences.

THEORIES OF SEX-ROLE DEVELOPMENT

Anthropologists in past decades used to uphold the theory that males have always been the dominant sex (Hays, 1972, reviewed in Forisha [1978], p. 43). In the study of sex roles, some researchers have emphasized certain sociological and biological influences over others. Historically, various theories have emerged to explain sex-role development. Four major theories are relevant to the study of sex-role behaviors: social-learning theory; cognitive developmental theory; identification (or Freudian) theory; and humanistic theory.

Much of the existing research on children's sex-role development has been based on a social-learning model. Along the lines of social-learning theory, Mischel (1966) labeled sex-typed activities as a function of one's entire social learning. He stressed the importance of environmental input into the sex-role learning process. Modelling, reward and punishment account for the social learning of sex role development in individuals; that is, females are rewarded for imitating the same-sex role models, and are likewise punished for demonstrating masculine behaviors (Bandura and Walters, 1963; Kagan, 1964; Mischel, 1974).

In contrast to the learning theory, those who support the ideas of cognitive development believe that gender identity comes first, which is followed by sex-appropriate behaviors (Kohlberg, 1966; Ullian, 1976; Katz, 1979). The child begins by recognizing gender differences between males and females, and then accepts the categories of masculine and feminine behaviors evident in society. Gender helps the child organize and categorize social perceptions, and sex-role expectations and behaviors. Socialization occurs when aspects of the child's social environment become thinking and action.

Kohlberg and Mischel are in general agreement about the broad outlines of the process of sex-role learning. These were cited by Miller and Reeves (1976, p. 37):

(a) children can learn from the appropriate behavior of both sexes through observation and without immediate reinforcement,

(b) children attempt to maximize benefits to themselves, i.e., feelings of self-worth for Kohlberg and reinforcement for Mischel, and

(c) this attempt causes children to emulate models of the same sex and/or models who have the power to gain rewards for themselves.

Proponents of the cognitive and social-learning theories see the difference between the two arguments as the extent to which the environment controls sex-role development. Freudian theorists who defend the idea of identification, however, believe that behavior is the result of psychological and physiological instincts (Hall and Lindzey, 1970). Freud believed that it is through the child's identification with the same-sex parent that he or she learns to be masculine or feminine (Flake-Hobson et al., 1980).

Humanists defend the concept of "self-socialization," a process which emphasizes the individuality of each person's life and experiences, as noted by Forisha (1978, p. 6):

They believe that although we are motivated by our inner impulses and shaped by our outer environment, we are essentially free to choose our own direction. Moreover, that direction, if well chosen, will not lead us into conflict with others, nor will it bring us rewards only at the expense of others. Rather, the humanists argue that humans who choose well benefit both themselves and society.

In a humanistic explanation of sex-role development, the individual may choose to incorporate information and behave in ways defined as masculine and/or feminine by the culture (Flake-Hobson et al., 1980, p. 158).

Currently, measurements of masculinity and femininity, as well as traditional conceptions of sex-role development, are undergoing a period of criticism and change (Williams, LaRose, and Frost, 1981, p. 5). The approach in theory being taken into account by sex-role researchers utilizes the humanist viewpoint. Maccoby and Jacklin (1974) emphasized this approach in their study of the psychology of sex differences:

Although biological factors are important in male-female differentiation, the available research findings most clearly support a self-socialization explanation of the development of sex differences in boys and girls.

Through self-socialization, the child first develops a concept of what it is to be male or female, and then, once he has a clear understanding of his own sex identity he attempts to fit his own behavior to his concept of what behavior is sex-appropriate.

STEREOTYPES AND TELEVISION CONTENT

Evidence from cross-cultural studies has determined that sex roles evolve from cultural influences (Tavris and Offir, 1977; Mead, 1950). These influences are instrumental in shaping and reflecting the sex-role stereotypes and images of the culture (Media Women's Association, 1974, reviewed in Kilbourne [1980]). Television is a prevalent medium in the presentation of sex-role stereotypes (Beuf, 1974). Several studies on television sex-role portrayals show that unrealistic, stereotyped sex roles permeate TV programming, and children's television in particular (Sternglanz and Serbin, 1974; Busby, 1974; Lemon, 1977).

A connection between traditional behaviors and the viewing of sex-role-stereotyped content has been demonstrated by Frueh and McGhee (1975). During their experiments with grade-school children, they concluded that high amounts of television viewing are associated with stronger traditional sex-role development in both boys and girls. Beuf (1974) has also provided evidence that there is a causal relationship between heavy television viewing and the development of more traditional sex-role beliefs in children; indeed, she found that children who watched more TV had a stronger traditional sex-role identity than did low television viewers.

Davidson, Yasuna, and Tower (1979) conducted a study to find out whether television has a direct effect on sex-role stereotyping in young girls. They exposed five- and six-year-old girls to three TV network cartoons—a non-traditional, reverse-stereotyped program, a neutral program, and a high-stereotyped program. Results showed significantly lower sex-role stereotyping scores after exposure to the non-traditional program than for the neutral and high-stereotyped program.

In 1964, DeFleur's content analysis of 250 TV shows found that the programming contained stereotyped beliefs and perceptions about a variety of occupations. He theorized that the untrue depictions on television may be reinforcing and perpetuating stereotyped ideas and incorrect generalizations. Later, DeFleur and DeFleur (1967) found that by the time a child is six years old, he or she will have already formed definite conceptions of occupational roles and of the social rankings among them. It follows that a child who views a great deal of television is much more likely to make a stereotyped occupational choice.

To measure the sex-related effects of stereotyped presentations, some researchers have used nonstereotypical portrayals in experimental studies (Scherer, 1970–71; Williams, LaRose and Frost, 1981; Miller and Reeves, 1976). Specific television content was linked to sex-role perception through a two-method approach in the work of Miller and Reeves (1976). First, they analyzed prime-time TV drama to isolate counter-stereotypical sex-role portrayals. Then, they constructed a survey to discover the impact of the counterstereotypical portrayals on children's occupational sex-role perceptions. According to the authors, their study supported the proposition that televised male and female role models have different appeals for boys and girls. Miller and Reeves established two reasons why the male and female children in their study chose different role models: There were more male characters to choose from; and male characters were more rewarded for their behavior and thus more appealing than female characters.

Miller and Reeves (1976, pp. 47–48) concluded:

> The findings support the assertion that television helps shape children's sex-role perceptions. Children do nominate television characters as people they want to be like when they grow up. There is ample evidence that children can learn through imitation and it is reasonable to assume that they will imitate particular people whom they say they want to be like.
>
> Since children choose primarily high stereotyped characters of their own sex, television must be directly teaching or reinforcing the stereotypes. The reasons boys and girls give for their model choices lends credence to this assertion. That is, boys often justify their choices on the basis of physical aggression attributes of models while girls justify their choices on the basis of physical attractiveness.
>
> . . . there is no explanation of why these differential levels of tolerance exist, except that male roles are in general more valued by society. If this interpretation is correct, it merely states that sex roles are stereotyped.

The research indicates that television does have an impact upon sex-role development in children. According to Comstock (1975), studies have shown that children develop definite tastes in television programming as early as age three, and that these tastes in programs are related to age and sex. Children also show marked sex differences in their use of media (Schramm et al., 1961). To assess the effects of TV's stereotyping on children, it is significant to review just how much television children are exposed to. Action for Children's Television (1981) offers these up-to-date statistics: The average American family watches more than six-and-a-half hours of television a day; children watch an average of 27 hours of TV each week, or almost four hours each day; and by the time they are 18, most children will have spent more time watching TV than being in school. Butler and Paisley (1980) believe that there is good cause for concern about the sex roles that children develop, considering the stereotyped nature of television content and the time children spend watching TV.

Monitoring the Medium: How Television Paints the Picture

The interpretation of sex roles in programs viewed by young people is the most widely researched aspect of the relationship among children, television, and sex-role stereotyping (Williams, LaRose, and Frost, 1981, p. 5). Over 45 content-analytic studies have examined sex-role images of men and women in television programs, and most of these analyses have been conducted since 1970. Less than half were content studies dealing primarily with character portrayals of sex roles in children's programs. This research reveals that TV shows designed for children display these trends:

1. Traditional sex roles permeate children's television-program content.
2. Sex-biased images are common in children's programs.
3. There are more male than female characters in both weekend and weekday children's TV.
4. Women are shown more often than men in family roles; men are shown in higher-status jobs.
5. Male characters are portrayed as knowledgeable, independent, and aggressive; female characters are shown as romantic, submissive, emotional, and timid.

Clark (1969, 1972) studied how different segments of the population achieve varying roles and statuses in the media. While describing the treatment that different groups received, Clark outlined stages of recognition and respect. Originated for examining media presentations of ethnic minorities, Clark's stages are also applicable to portrayals of males and females on television. "Recognition" refers to the frequency of a particular group's appearance on TV (or in other media). "Respect" refers to the type of portrayals that the group is given. Recognition and respect are assigned to the characters of television programs in different ways. The stages can be looked at in terms of proportions of male and female characters and their assignment to various occupations and dramatic roles; and the kinds of personality characteristics and behaviors exhibited by male and female characters. The following content studies reveal some aspects of the types of treatment—the roles and statuses—achieved by male and female characters in television content directed at the child audience.

Studies of Sex Roles in Programs Directed at Children

Sternglanz and Serbin (1974) performed an observational analysis of the male and female role models presented on ten popular commercially produced children's television programs. They chose programs that were reported to be among the most popular children's programs during the 1971–72 season, based on Nielson ratings. Their research revealed, first, striking sex differences in the number of male and female roles portrayed and in the behaviors of male and female characters. Second, males were more often portrayed as aggressive and constructive (e.g., building and planning) than were females. Females were more likely to be shown as deferent. Third, the consequences of behavior were different, with males more often being rewarded. An exception was that females were more often punished for high levels of activity than were males. The results of their study showed that there were more than twice as many male roles in commercially produced children's programs; that females were shown in traditional occupational roles; and that female characters possessed, to a greater degree, certain personality attributes generally associated with being female (i.e., deference and nurturance) than did the male characters.

Long and Simon (1974) looked specifically at how women are portrayed on children and family programs. The study described the amount of time women were on the screen; statuses held and roles played by women; the nature of female/male interactions; and the physical characteristics of the females portrayed in the programs. Their conclusions included these points: Women were portrayed in comic roles or as wives and mothers in a family context; none were married and working outside the home simultaneously. Dominant characteristics of females were subservience, dependence upon others, and less rational behavior than was shown by male counterparts. Women held no positions of authority, were silly and overemotional; and tended to look alike—well groomed, almost always under 40 years of age, attractive, and concerned with their appearance.

Studies sponsored by Action for Children's Television monitored the portrayals of sexual images in children's programs at various time periods during the 1970s. In an analysis of the content of commercial children's television programs broadcast on weekends and weekday afternoons, 899 characters were classified (Barcus, 1978a). The study revealed that male characters outnumbered females by a 3:1 margin. Males dominated all age categories, and male adults on weekend programs outnumbered female adults by 4:1 (245 males; 60 females). These figures were almost exact replicas of the ratios for males and females on children's weekend and weekday programs three years earlier (Barcus, 1975 a,b). When analyzed by program format in 1978, the male/female distribution pattern was similar, with the exception of informational-type programs, in which the ratio was not as extreme (5:3). In all other categories, male characters ranged from 63 percent to 88 percent of the total.

Nolan, Galst, and White (1977) also examined the sexes on children's television programs that were aired on Saturday mornings. They isolated sex-differentiated patterns of verbal approval and disapproval on 20 hours of programs that were observed over a four-week period. A summary of their study (1977, p. 197) explains what they discovered:

> Males outnumbered females on screen by a ratio of three to one, and they gave and received higher rates of approval and disapproval. Even when rates of received approval per person were balanced by sex, males gave significantly higher rates of approval and disapproval and received significantly higher rates of disapproval. Males differed from females in the types and range of behaviors for which they received approval or disapproval.

Nolan et al. (p. 203) concluded that:

1. Children are receiving much greater exposure to male models during Saturday morning television.
2. Those male models are more frequently shown to be in the position of power than females, for it is they who bestow significantly more verbal reinforcements.

These researchers believe that their data illustrate this lesson for children: that boys are more significant persons than girls.

Busby (1974) studied commercial network programs directed at children and found that they portrayed traditional male and female social roles. Busby examined the sex-role standard presented in commercial network programs directed toward children; and whether or not the sex-role standard could be anticipated by examining the nature of commercial television programming influences and traditional attitudinal postures concerning male and female roles in society.

Busby used 40 items to distinguish differences between the sexes. She discovered that males were braver, stronger, and more aggressive, while females were less knowledgeable, less independent, and less dominant. Busby found that in the commercial network children's programs, males dominated in the home and in society. She stated (1974, p. 696), "A sex-role standard is being presented in the programs that can be divided along the lines of traditional sex-role understandings, with males assuming complete responsibility for family financial support, and the females assuming responsibility for child care and routine home maintenance."

Streicher (1974) examined the image of females in cartoons aired on Saturdays, Sundays, and weekday afternoons. What Streicher (p. 127) found was:

> In general, cartoon females were less numerous than males, made fewer appearances, had fewer lines, played fewer "lead roles," were less noisy, and were more preponderantly juvenile than males. Mothers worked only in the house; males did not participate in housework. In many activities in which girls showed some form of skill (e.g., cheerleading), their performance was duplicated by a dog or other pet. Other stereotypes appeared. The female who really had a *lot* was Maid Marian, Robin Hoodnick's girl, who was constantly nagging, complaining, wanting, talking, until someone put a bag over her head.

According to Streicher, when a female did appear in a cartoon, her lines were of the "Help! Save me!" variety.

Mayes and Valentine (1979, p. 41) studied whether or not children perceive sex-role stereotyping in Saturday-morning cartoon shows; they defined stereotypical sex roles as:

> . . . a collection of traditional norms (sex-typed attributes) that differentiate typical feminine behavior patterns from typical masculine behavior patterns in contemporary American society. For example, a stereotypical female in a cartoon would tend to be helpless; while a stereotypical male would tend to solve problems.

In the process of selecting the cartoons for the study, Mayes and Valentine found that males significantly outnumbered female characters in most Saturday-morning cartoon shows, and that some of the programs had no female characters at all. So they chose to examine those cartoon shows on the three commercial networks that contained a significant amount of dialogue spoken by female characters. They narrowed the programs down to four. The evaluation of characters was based on 14 personality attributes, to discover which ones were markedly different for males and females. The study provided evidence that child viewers perceived that the characters they viewed possessed sex-typed attributes; according to the children's evaluations, the characters clearly exhibited stereotypical sex-role behaviors.

Levinson (1975) also studied the sex-role-stereotypical nature of television cartoon programs. This research considered the frequencies of male and female characters in televised cartoons, as well as their occupational roles and the dramatic context in which they were portrayed. Levinson found:

1. Males outnumbered females three to one, and were seen in a greater variety of roles, as well.

2. Females were defined in terms of status in relation to males, and were most commonly portrayed as pretty teenage girls or adult housewives.
3. Adult women were rarely portrayed.
4. The careers of females were limited to the traditionally feminine-stereotyped occupations, i.e., secretary, teacher.
5. Women were seen as dumb, spiteful, catty, or the sweet and faithful girlfriend, while males were stable and intelligent beings.
6. If the characters were married, the men worked, but the women never worked.

In general, the cartoons presented females as passive performers of "socioemotional" roles as compared to the males' "instrumental" roles; females were defined in status by their relationship to males, and rarely initiated action or performed tasks of physical strength or bravado. According to Levinson, female characters were stereotyped—the pretty, dumb girl (e.g., Melody in "Josie and the Pussycats"; Raquel Wallflower in "The Flintstones," also voted the dumbest girl in school); the "superbrain" (e.g., Bella in "Scooby Doo" and Moon Rock in "The Flintstones," who both wore eyeglasses); and the spiteful, catty type (e.g., Alexandria of "Josie and the Pussycats"). Males, too, had exaggerated characteristics but were much more likely to be portrayed as stable, intelligent beings without what Levinson refers to as a "burlesqued character weakness."

Shechtman (1978) assessed the distribution of male-versus-female occupational portrayals in terms of occupational prestige on the following six television shows most frequently mentioned by preschool children: "Batman," "Bugs Bunny," "Sesame Street," "Flintstones," "Happy Days," and "Road Runner." Shechtman divided occupations into four ranges of occupational prestige, to explore patterns of the distribution of occupational portrayals. He used these four prestige groups: high, 85–100 (e.g., inventor, doctor); medium, 70–84 (e.g., athlete, teacher); low, 55–69 (e.g., crane operator, singer); below 54 (e.g., laborer, lumberjack).

From his research, he concluded that television, as a source of incidental learning, offers the child a male-dominated picture of the occupational world. Shechtman's findings indicate that women are portrayed in inferior occupational roles and in proportions not representing real-world numbers. He outlined the results of his study:

1. Men outnumbered women in all occupational prestige categories, with six males to every female.
2. On educational shows ("Sesame Street") men outnumbered women in all occupational prestige categories, with seven males to every female.
3. No women were portrayed in the high-level (85–100) occupational prestige category on any of the six shows.

4. Men outnumbered women in all other levels of occupational prestige:

Medium level—10 males to every female
Low level—4 males to each female
Below 54—27 males to every female.

Additional research by Shechtman (1978) provides some insight into the relationship of career awareness, television, and preschool children. His findings showed the following:

Ninety-five percent of the children named an occupational choice for adulthood. There was a strong relationship between occupational choice prestige levels of boys and girls with the occupational-prestige level of their favorite television character's occupation. There were stronger correlations between the occupational-prestige levels of boys and girls with their favorite television character than with their same-sex parent.

Summary

This review of past research has shown consistent findings with respect to sex-role learning and sex-role portrayals on television: Children do learn sex-role behaviors through observation and imitation of TV role models. Further, in children's television, female role models are underrepresented by a wide margin overall, and especially in meaningful major dramatic and occupational roles. And both male and female role models in children's television engage in rigid sex-role behaviors and display traditional and stereotyped male or female personality traits.

5 RECOGNITION OF THE SEXES

In Chapter 3 a preview of the dominance of males in children's TV was seen in the groupings of male and female characters in the program segments, and in the tendency for single-sex groupings of males. Whereas 35 percent of all segments contained only male characters, about 2 percent had only females.

In this chapter the basic sex distributions of all characters are analyzed by age group, racial and ethnic classifications, marital status, and family role.

For all 1,145 characters coded in the study, slightly more than three-fourths were male, about one-fifth were female, and the remainder not classifiable by sex (see Table 5.1). Thus, of those classified, 78 percent were male and 22 percent were female (the 38 characters not classified as to sex are eliminated from the analysis in the remainder of this study).

Females were also more likely to be cast in human roles, as compared with animal or other nonhuman roles (see Table 5.2). That is, of 243 female characters, 83.5 percent were cast as humans, compared with 64.2 percent of 864 male characters. Looked at another way, 27

Table 5.1 Distribution of the Sexes, All Characters

SEX	NUMBER	PERCENT
Males	864	75.5
Females	243	21.2
Unclassifiable	38	3.3
Total	1,145	100.0

Table 5.2   Distribution of Characters, by Type and Sex

TYPE	MALE	FEMALE	PERCENT FEMALE
Humans	64.2%	83.5%	27
Animals	25.6	9.5	9
Other nonhumans	10.2	7.0	16
Total (percent)	100.0	100.0	
Total (number)	(864)	(243)	22

Note: Percentages in the tables in this chapter are presented two ways. In the "Male" and "Female" columns, percents are computed vertically and are always based on the total number of males or females in each column. Thus, in this table, of 864 male characters (which is 100 percent of all males), 64.2 percent were humans; 25.6 percent, animals; and 10.2 percent, other nonhuman characters such as robots. The "Percent Female" column shows the percent of all humans, animals, or other nonhumans who are female. Each of these figures can be compared with the percent of all characters who are female (i.e., 22 percent of 1,107 total characters classifiable by sex). Thus, 27 percent of all humans were female, but only 9 percent of animal characters were female.

percent of all human characters were female; this compares with 22 percent of all characters. For some reason, animals are seldom cast as female characters; only 9 percent of animals were identified, through dress or voice, as female.

SEX AND AGE OF THE CHARACTERS

Female characters appear as younger than males (see Table 5.3). Although there were more males than females in every age category, there were proportionately larger percentages of female teens and young adults (64 percent combined) than there were of males in these groups (44 percent). The middle-aged female is the most underrepresented character, although proportionately more females are shown in elderly roles. Females constituted 43 percent of all teens, 39 percent of the elderly, and 31 percent of young adults, all of which are in higher ratios than females are of the total (22 percent). The ratio of male-to-female child characters is about the same as the ratio for the total population.

SEX, MARITAL STATUS, AND FAMILY ROLE

Females were identified more often as married individuals than were males. Many characters appeared as unattached adults, but, to be classified as single (children and teens were not coded), there had to be

Table 5.3 Distribution of the Sexes, by Age Group

GROUP	MALE	FEMALE	PERCENT FEMALE
Children	15.0%	11.8%	22
Teens	10.1	20.7	43
Young adults	34.1	42.9	31
Middle-aged persons	37.0	18.0	15
Elderly	3.8	6.6	39
Total (percent)	100.0	100.0	
Total (number)	(581)	(212)	27

Note: Data exclude many animal and nonhuman characters unclassifiable by age.

some clear indication that the single individual was looking for or dating the opposite sex, or otherwise identified as of single status. Therefore, only 194 characters were identified as definitely single, married, or widowed. Interestingly, females were much more often identified both as to single or married status (35 percent of females as compared with only 13 percent of males). In addition, when marital status was shown, females were more often identified as married, and the only characters identified as widowed were three women (see Table 5.4).

Females were more apt to be cast in family or kinship roles as well (see Table 5.5). There were 263 characters identified in family and kinship roles. Of these, 38 percent were female as compared to nonfamily roles, in which only 17 percent were female. Females were more apt to be cast as grandmothers, mothers, and wives than were males in their familial counterpart roles.

Sex by Race and Ethnicity

By racial classification (human characters only), males again dominated each category, although there was a slightly greater proportion of

Table 5.4 Distribution of the Sexes, by Marital Status

STATUS	MALE	FEMALE	PERCENT FEMALE
Single	50.9%	44.0%	40
Married	49.1	52.4	45
Widowed	—	3.6	100
Total (percent)	100.0	100.0	
Total (number)	(110)	(84)	43

Note: Data exclude children and teens and others not clearly identified as either single or married.

Table 5.5 Sex Distributions by Family-Role Assignments

FAMILY ROLE	MALE	FEMALE	PERCENT FEMALE
Parents (fathers, mothers)	33.1%	39.0%	42
Children (sons, daughters)	40.5	35.0	35
Spouses (husbands, wives)	8.6	11.0	44
Siblings (brothers, sisters)	6.2	6.0	38
Grandparents (grandfathers, grandmothers)	0.6	3.0	75
Others (uncles, aunts)	4.3	3.0	30
Others (nephews, nieces)	5.5	2.0	18
Others (cousins)	1.2	1.0	33
Total (percent)	100.0	100.0	
Total (number)	(163)	(100)	38
Nonfamily roles	(701)	(143)	17

females among blacks than among whites or other minorities (see Table 5.6).*

All characters were also classified according to ethnic origins. Although the 184 ethnically identified characters did not differ in the male-female ratio from 923 nonethnic characters, there were some differences in specific ethnic classifications. Blacks (U.S. and non-American blacks) had a larger proportion of females than any other group, whereas Europeans (including the English, Irish, Germans, French, Italians, and Slavics) and Arabs were especially dominated by males (see Table 5.7).

Table 5.6 Distribution of the Sexes, by Racial Classification (human characters only)

RACE	MALE	FEMALE	PERCENT FEMALE
White	87.0%	86.7%	27
Black	5.1	6.4	32
Other minorities	6.3	5.9	26
Uncertain	1.6	1.0	18
Total (percent)	100.0	100.0	
Total (number)	(555)	(203)	27

---

*"Race" is used to classify only human characters into three groups—white, black, and other minorities. "Ethnicity" is used to classify all characters by national origin or on the basis of accent, surname, dress, or locale.

Table 5.7 Distribution of the Sexes by Ethnicity

GROUP	MALES	FEMALES	PERCENT FEMALE
Blacks	19.9%	34.2%	31
Europeans	45.2	28.9	14
Arabs	7.5	5.3	15
Asians	4.8	5.3	22
Hispanics	18.5	21.0	23
Other ethnics	4.1	5.3	25
Total (percent)	100.0	100.0	
Total (number)	(146)	(38)	21
Not identified			
ethnically	(718)	(205)	22

Sex Distributions in Various Program Types

Approximately 70 percent of all characters classified in the study appear in cartoon comedies and action/adventure dramas. In these categories females are outnumbered by 4:1, whereas in other comedy dramas (nonanimated), in miscellaneous other dramas, and in informational programs, they are proportionately better represented, although still outnumbered by about 7:3 (see Table 5.8).

Summary

There is an absolute and consistent male dominance among characters in commercial children's television—whether in comedy, adventure, or other programs; in all age groups; in various racial and ethnic groups; and in different family roles.

Relative to males, however, females tend to be portrayed as younger, more likely to be married or widowed, and more likely to be found in family roles (primarily as wives, mothers, and grandmothers).

Table 5.8 Sex Distributions in Various Program Types

PROGRAM TYPE	MALES	FEMALES	PERCENT FEMALE
Cartoon comedy	51.4%	44.5%	20
Other comedy	3.4	5.4	31
Action/adventure drama	21.6	18.5	19
Other drama	6.9	11.1	31
Other entertainment	1.4	1.2	20
Informational	15.3	19.3	26
Total (percent)	100.0	100.0	
Total (number)	(864)	(243)	22

A higher percentage of black characters are females, as compared to whites, and to other racial and ethnic groups.

We have presented the general picture of the distribution in the ratio of males to females. The next question to be addressed is the relative importance of the female and male roles; this analysis appears in Chapter 6.

6 THE TREATMENT OF THE SEXES

As stated in the Introduction, content measures of respect are indicated by the treatment of various groups in the programs. One measure is the assignment of characters to major and minor roles. Other measures include the social class, working status, and occupational roles of the characters.

SEX AND DRAMATIC ROLES

Both in absolute numbers and in proportion to their totals, males are assigned more major roles in the stories than are females (see Table 6.1). Whereas more than one-half of all males played major roles in the programs, only four in ten females did so. Females were most frequently found in submajor roles with little responsibility for the outcomes of the stories, in helping and supporting positions, and without sufficient character development to clearly identify them in terms of their goals or personality traits. They were outnumbered by approximately 9:1 in both hero and villain roles, and by 4:1 in other major character roles.

Females constituted 22 percent of all characters. They were only 17 percent of all major characters and 16 percent of all major dramatic characters, yet constituted 27 percent of minor characters.

Employment Status and Occupational Roles

Of all characters coded for sex and working status, 39 percent could be identified as employed in gainful occupations. For males, 42 percent

Table 6.1   Role Importance of Characters, by Sex

ROLE	MALES	FEMALES	PERCENT FEMALE
Dramatic heroes	10.9%	5.3%	12
Dramatic villains	9.5	2.5	7
Other major dramatic characters	25.4	23.1	20
Total, dramatic characters	45.8	30.9	16
Major nondramatic	9.0	9.0	22
Total, major characters	54.9	39.9	17
Submajor characters	23.5	38.3	31
Minor characters	21.6	21.8	22
Total, minor characters	45.1	60.1	27
All characters (percent)	100.0	100.0	
All characters (number)	(864)	(243)	22

were so employed; for females, only 29 percent were. To state it another way, only 16 percent of 429 working characters were female.

By occupation, the variety of occupations assigned women was considerably more limited than those for men. There were no female operatives, transport-equipment workers, laborers, or farmers; and only one female sales worker and one craftsperson. In proportion to their totals, females were extremely outnumbered in all occupational roles except for clerical workers, household workers, students, and homemakers, in which the female ratio was higher than for each of the other occupational groups (see Table 6.2).

For both men and women, the largest percentages of all occupational roles were found in the professional and technical class—including not only doctors, lawyers, teachers, and scientists, but also professional musicians and other entertainers. When looked at closely by subgroup, one finds that female professionals were cast primarily as entertainers (69 percent of female professionals as compared with 58 percent of male professionals). In more prestigious professional occupations, males dominated. Whereas there were a number of male scientists, inventors, doctors, and pilots, there were only three women scientists, one female technician, and one social scientist. In addition, women comprised seven of the 11 teachers.

In the nonentertainment/mass-media-related professional occupations, males outnumbered females by more than 4:1, whereas in entertainment-related occupations, the ratio was about 7:3.

A complete list of occupations is provided in Table 6.3. Although eight females were classified in managerial roles, only three were what might be termed "normal" managers (business heads, for example). The remainder were royalty (princesses and queens) and one Amazon

Table 6.2 Occupational Roles of the Characters, by Sex

OCCUPATIONAL ROLE	ALL CATEGORIES		INCOME PRODUCING ONLY		PERCENT FEMALE
	MALE	FEMALE	MALE	FEMALE	
Professional and technical	17.8%	19.8%	42.9%	68.6%	24
Managerial	6.8	3.3	16.4	11.4	12
Sales workers	0.8	0.4	2.0	1.4	12
Clerical	0.4	1.2	0.8	4.3	50
Craftsmen	2.1	0.4	5.0	1.4	5
Operatives	2.8	—	6.7	—	0
Transport-equipment operatives	0.9	—	2.2	—	0
Laborers	0.6	—	1.4	—	0
Farmers and farm labor	0.2	—	0.6	—	0
Service workers	7.9	1.2	18.9	4.3	4
Household workers	1.3	2.5	3.1	8.6	35
Students	1.6	4.5			44
Homemakers	—	6.6			100
Retired	0.2	—			0
Illegal occupations	3.8	1.7			11
Employed, but occupation uncertain	0.7	0.4			14
Not shown as employed	52.1	58.0			24
Total (percent)	100.0	100.0	100.0	100.0	
Total (number)	(864)	(243)	(359)	(70)	22

leader.* Women were not found as political leaders (except for the Amazon), nor in law-enforcement, military, educational, or other managerial positions. They were even denied participation in most illegal occupational roles.

Sex and Social Class

Somewhat predictably (given the occupational analysis), social-class data show all characters concentrated in the upper- and lower-middle classes, with females proportionately more prominent in lower-middle and males in upper-middle classes. Males dominated the upper and lower classes as well as the déclassé category; only female elites (primarily royalty) were on a par with men (see Table 6.4).

---

*These characters caused a problem in coding. Although included in the managerial class, as are many political leaders in the census classifications, perhaps a separate category should have been established for royalty.

Table 6.3   List of Male and Female Occupations

OCCUPATION	MALE	FEMALE
Professional, Technical, and Kindred Workers		
Circus entertainers		
clown	2	—
strongman	2	—
ringmaster	2	—
carnival barker	2	—
circus performer	1	1
mummy	1	—
lion tamer	1	—
circus owner/entertainer	1	—
Other entertainers		
TV-show host	12	4
actor	8	1
master of ceremonies	4	—
game-show host	2	—
TV advice giver	1	2
magician	1	—
entertainer	1	1
model	—	1
Music related		
musician	8	14
singer/song writer	2	—
orchestra conductor	2	—
opera singer	1	1
singer	1	—
piano player	1	—
violin player	1	—
bandleader	1	—
singer/dancer	—	1
Sports related		
gymnast	3	—
hockey player	1	—
boxer	1	—
athletic coach	1	—
boxing referee	1	—
racing official	1	—
bullfight announcer	1	—
matador	1	—
Media personnel		
newspaper editor	3	—
news commentator	2	3
animator	2	1
TV reporter	2	—
publicity agent	2	—
author/illustrator	2	—
newspaper reporter	1	3

Table 6.3 List of Male and Female Occupations (cont.)

OCCUPATION	MALE	FEMALE
newscaster	1	—
sports commentator	1	—
movie producer	1	—
TV producer	1	—
cameraman	1	—
author/professional runner	1	—
disk jockey	1	—
Science/Engineering		
scientist	11	2
inventor/scientist	3	—
engineer	2	—
astronomer	1	1
architect	1	—
surveyor	1	—
marine specialist	1	—
botanist	1	—
Technicians		
airplane pilot	14	—
pilot of robot jet	3	—
astronaut	2	—
air-traffic controller	1	—
radar operator	—	1
Doctors		
doctor	6	1
surgeon	1	—
Social scientists		
psychiatrist	1	—
social worker	1	—
counsellor	1	1
Lawyers/judges		
lawyers	1	—
judges	1	—
Religious workers		
high priest	1	—
Teachers		
music instructor	1	—
muscle building instructor	1	—
professor	1	—
school teachers	—	5
boarding-school teachers	—	2
Managers and administrators except farm		
Royalty		
king	1	—
king of cat people	1	—
sire (leader of knights)	1	—
princess	—	1

Table 6.3 List of Male and Female Occupations (cont.)

OCCUPATION	MALE	FEMALE
queen of wonderland	—	1
queen of Egypt	—	1
queen of cat people	—	1
Political leaders		
mayor	7	—
leader of an empire	2	—
Gamelon leader	2	—
African official	1	—
African ambassador	1	—
Senate majority leader	1	—
leader of man apes	1	—
leader of monkey people	1	—
Amazon leader	—	1
Law related		
police commissioner	3	—
police captain	2	—
police chief	1	—
police superintendent	1	—
superintendent of "Ireland" Yard	1	—
Military leaders		
commander	4	—
general	1	—
head of international rescue	1	—
Private businesses		
businessman	3	—
head of a big company	1	1
hotel manager	1	—
manager of a zoological foundation	1	—
opera-house manager	1	—
bank manager	1	—
zoo keeper	1	—
director of a training center	1	—
fruitstand owner	1	—
cafe manager	1	—
pizza-business owner	1	—
financial manager	1	—
restaurant owner	—	1
bakery owner	—	1
Ships		
captain	7	—
Educational		
school principal	1	—
head of a boarding school	1	—
Miscellaneous		
head of some organization	1	—

Table 6.3 List of Male and Female Occupations (cont.)

OCCUPATION	MALE	FEMALE
Sales workers		
grocery-store clerk	2	—
candy-store clerk	1	—
sales clerk	1	1
cap peddler	1	—
paper boy	1	—
sales representative	1	—
Clerical and kindred workers		
hotel desk clerk	2	—
mailman	1	—
switchboard operator	—	3
Craftsmen and kindred workers		
Tradesmen (skilled)		
clock repairman	3	—
plumber	2	—
shoe repairman	1	—
fix-it-shop man	1	—
printing-press operator	1	—
spaceship mechanic	1	—
construction worker	1	—
carpenter	1	—
blacksmith	1	—
Military		
soldier	6	2
Operatives except transport		
sailor	16	—
ship crew member	4	—
deckhand	2	—
painter	2	—
seaman	1	—
Transport-equipment operatives		
railroad worker	2	—
rickshaw puller	1	—
river guide	1	—
taxi driver	1	—
toll collector	1	—
truck driver	1	—
Laborers except farm		
construction laborer	2	—
lion feeder	1	—
animal caretaker	1	—
assistant to zoo keeper	1	—
Farmers and farm managers		
rancher	1	—
Farm laborers and farm foreman		
laborer	1	—

Table 6.3   List of Male and Female Occupations (cont.)

OCCUPATION	MALE	FEMALE
Service workers, except private-household ones		
Cleaning		
janitor	2	—
Food		
cook	3	—
busboy	2	—
soda-fountain jerk	1	—
waiter	1	1
bartender	1	—
gourmet cook/caterer	1	—
Health		
exterminator (mouser)	2	—
exterminator (Pied Piper)	1	—
Personal		
mental-hospital attendant	2	—
barber	1	—
lighthouse keeper	1	—
tour guide	1	1
elevator operator	1	—
boardinghouse person	—	1
Protective		
policeman	26	—
police sergeant	10	—
detective	3	—
spy	2	—
sheriff	1	—
security guard	1	—
night watchman	1	—
park ranger	1	—
police trainee	1	—
Private-household workers		
butler	6	—
cook	2	—
servant	2	1
queen's assistant	1	—
housekeeper	—	2
robot maid	—	2
babysitter	—	1
Students	14	11
Homemakers	—	17
Retired		
grandfather	1	—
circus performer	1	—
Illegal occupations (lawbreakers, robbers, etc.)		
Realistic		
crook/thief	4	—

Table 6.3   List of Male and Female Occupations (cont.)

OCCUPATION	MALE	FEMALE
kidnapper	3	—
cattle thief	3	—
pirate	3	—
swindler	2	—
spy	2	—
blackmailer	1	—
bank robber	1	—
burglar	1	—
gold thief	1	—
robber-baron	1	—
criminal (driver)	1	—
Fictional		
flying demon	1	—
evildoer	1	—
phantom of the opera	1	—
hippo-hypnotist	1	—
candy bandit	1	—
animal master	—	1
criminal (cat woman)	—	1
Assistants		
assistant to evildoer	2	1
worker for blackmailer	2	—
assistant to hypnotist	1	—
assistant to cattle thief	1	—
assistant to candy bandit	1	—

Table 6.4   Social Class of Characters, by Sex

CLASS	MALE	FEMALE	PERCENT FEMALE
Elite	1.9%	7.5%	50
Upper	5.8	4.7	17
Upper-middle	44.9	42.5	20
Lower-middle	31.6	39.6	24
Lower	5.3	1.9	8
Déclassé	10.5	3.8	9
Total (percent)	100.0	100.0	
Total (number)	(412)	(106)	20

Summary

This analysis has shown that female characters in children's TV not only are greatly outnumbered in nearly all but biologically defined female roles; they are also dominated with regard to their treatment in assignment to respectful roles. They are less apt to be assigned major roles (especially hero and villain roles); they are less likely to work; and when they work, not only are their opportunities limited, but they are assigned less prestigious and socially meaningful occupations.

7 VALUE ORIENTATIONS OF MALES AND FEMALES: GOALS AND MEANS TO GOALS

Value orientations are seen in the goals characters seek and the mean, by which they attempt to achieve their goals. Of the 490 major dramatic characters included in the study, 447 could be classed as to both sex and goal orientations. These 447 constitute the sample of characters analyzed in this chapter.

The analysis of goal orientations, grouped into self-goals and altruistic goals in Table 7.1, provides some interesting distinctions between female and male characters. Overall, female characters seek more altruistic goals than do males. Whereas nearly one-half of males sought self-goals, less than one-third of females did so.

For all characters, justice/duty and love/affection goals were most common, followed by self-indulgence and self-preservation goals. However, there were definite female/male differences with respect to these and other goal orientations. Relatively speaking, male self-goals were headed by self-indulgence, wealth, and expressions of hatred, whereas for females, self-preservation was the number-one self-goal. This finding supports previous findings that women are more vulnerable and more likely to be the victims of threats or violence.

For altruistic goals, the proportions of females exceed males slightly in justice/duty and love/affection goals, but much more so in home/family goals.

Overall, coders reported that goal assignments for females were more difficult tasks than for males—primarily because the expression of their goals was not as clearly presented. Thus, there was a larger proportion of miscellaneous altruistic goals sought by females (e.g., those involving idealism, respect for others, freedom, aesthetic goals, morality, and religion).

Table 7.1   Major Goals of Dramatic Characters, by Sex

GOAL CATEGORY	MALE	FEMALE	PERCENT FEMALE*
Self-Goals			
Self-indulgence (satisfaction of impulse, leisure, escape)	12.9%	4.5%	6
Self-preservation (safety)	7.6	14.9	26
Wealth (material success)	10.0	3.0	5
Hatred (revenge, destruction, spite)	8.4	—	0
Fame (reputation, prestige, popularity)	3.9	1.5	6
Power (mastery over others)	2.9	4.5	21
Thrill (adventure, pleasure)	2.9	1.5	8
Other self-goals	1.1	—	0
Total, self-goals	49.7	29.9	10
Altruistic Goals			
Justice (duty, preservation of law and order)	17.4	19.4	16
Love (friendship, companionship, affection)	14.0	16.4	17
Work (industriousness)	4.2	3.0	11
Home (marriage, family, parental duties)	2.6	8.9	37
Patriotism (devotion to country)	3.4	1.5	7
Knowledge (education, enlightenment)	2.4	3.0	18
Devotion to a cause or group	2.1	3.0	20
Other altruistic goals (respect for others, aesthetic values, idealism, brotherhood, etc.)	4.2	14.9	38
Total, altruistic goals	50.3	70.1	20
Total (percent)	100.0	100.0	
Total (number)	(380)	(67)	15

*As in the previous chapters, tables include the "percent female" column to provide an additional perspective as to the relative importance of each goal category to female characters. Thus, females constituted 15 percent of all major dramatic characters; they were only 6 percent of all characters seeking self-indulgence, 26 percent of those seeking self-preservation, and so forth.

Interestingly, females attained their goals more frequently than did males—especially their self-goals. What this probably reflects is that, because of different goal orientations, male goals of hatred/revenge, self-indulgence, wealth, and fame were more often blocked or not achieved, whereas female self-preservation goals were often achieved (see Table 7.2).

Table 7.2   The Attainment of Goals, by Sex

| | PERCENT OF GOALS ACHIEVED | |
CATEGORY	MALES	FEMALES
Self-goals	36	75
Altruistic goals	74	81
Total, all goals	56	79

GOAL-SEEKING BEHAVIORS

In attempting to achieve their goals, males exceeded females by far in the use of violence and trickery/deceit. Females, on the other hand, attempted to accomplish goals more frequently through dependence on others, the use of personal charm, and reliance on constituted authority (see Table 7.3). Thus, while females constituted only 15 percent of major dramatic characters, they were 47 percent of all characters utilizing personal charm in achieving goals.

Goal-seeking behavior was different for self- and altruistic-goal seeking (see Table 7.4). Violence was more frequently utilized by male characters in self-goal seeking, whereas females achieved self-goals through dependence on others. Both sexes relied heavily on personal industry and planning to achieve altruistic goals, but males used violence to a much greater extent in seeking altruistic goals. Females, on the other hand, used personal charm, dependence on others, and constituted authority to a greater extent than did males.

Table 7.3   Goal-Seeking Behaviors, by Sex

MEANS USED	MALES	FEMALES	PERCENT FEMALE
Violence	32.8%	10.8%	6
Authority (law, police)	5.0	9.2	25
Luck/fate/chance	5.2	6.2	17
Trickery/deceit	12.4	3.1	4
Personal charm	2.2	10.7	47
Persuasion	4.1	3.1	12
Dependence on others	7.4	21.5	34
Personal industry/intelligence	25.4	29.2	17
Other means	5.5	6.2	17
Total (percent)	100.0	100.0	
Total (number)	(363)	(65)	15

Table 7.4   Means Used in Seeking Self- and Altruistic Goals, by Sex

	SELF-GOALS		ALTRUISTIC GOALS	
MEANS USED	MALE	FEMALES	MALE	FEMALES
Violence	44.8%	18.8%	21.7%	8.2%
Authority	2.3	—	7.4	12.2
Luck/fate/chance	4.0	12.5	6.3	4.1
Trickery/deceit	21.3	6.3	4.2	2.0
Personal charm	1.7	—	2.7	14.3
Persuasion	4.6	—	3.7	4.1
Dependence on others	6.9	50.0	7.9	12.3
Personal industry	12.1	6.2	37.6	36.7
Other means	2.3	6.2	8.5	6.1
Total (percent)	100.0	100.0	100.0	100.0
Total (number)	(174)	(16)	(189)	(49)

Barriers to Achievement of Goals

What were the primary barriers to achieving goals? Primarily, it was violence. Female goal seeking, however, was more often opposed by violence than was male goal seeking (see Table 7.5).

Table 7.5   Barriers to Goals, by Sex

BARRIER	MALES	FEMALES	PERCENT FEMALE
Violence	51.7%	60.9%	16
Authority	4.5	—	0
Luck/fate/chance	9.9	6.5	9
Trickery/deceit	9.3	6.5	10
Personal charm	—	—	—
Persuasion	0.7	2.2	33
Personal deficiencies	7.5	2.2	4
Personal industry	12.3	8.7	10
Other barriers	4.1	13.0	33
Total (percent)	100.0	100.0	
Total (number)	(292)	(46)	14

Note: Barriers were defined, in most cases, as actions taken by others in blocking goal achievement. The exceptions were luck, fate or chance, and the character's own personal deficiencies, such as stupidity or clumsiness.

Summary

Females appear to be upholding many of the traditional values in society in children's television. Males, on the other hand, seem more devoted to self-seeking goals and behaviors. Females are more likely to seek altruistic goals and are more likely to achieve them. More specifically, however, it was found that females are more apt to seek love, home, and family goals, and are more concerned with self-preservation. Males, on the other hand, were more apt to be self-indulgent, seek wealth, act out of hatred or revenge, and devote themselves to work and patriotic goals.

As to goal-seeking means, both males and females utilized personal industry or intelligent planning to a considerable extent, whereas males were much more likely to utilize violence or trickery. Females, on the other hand, often depended on others or utilized personal charm in attempts to accomplish their goals. This pattern was true whether self- or altruistic goals were being sought, although violent means were much more often utilized for self- than for other goals. Violence was also the major barrier to be overcome—especially for females.

8 SEX-ROLE BEHAVIORS AND PERSONALITY TRAITS

In this chapter sex-role portrayals are examined by means of two separate measures. The first is an analysis of what are called sex-role attributes—those behaviors that have been found to represent traditional sex-role training of female and male children in society. Secondly, personality scales are utilized to measure differences in the selected personality traits of the characters.

Sex-Role Attributes

The sex-role attribute scales utilized in the study were adapted from the work of Jeanne Block, of the Department of Psychology, University of California, and reported in the "Nova" program "The Pinks and the Blues," originally broadcast on PBS in September 1980. According to her research, from the time of birth, boys and girls are taught sex-role behaviors, often in subtle and unconscious ways, beginning with the pink-and-blue clothing provided in the first days of life. Through the observation and study of parents and teachers and the manners in which they influence the socialization of children, she listed eight different areas (summarized here from a transcript of "The Pinks and the Blues," PBS, September 1980) that distinguish male and female sex-role behaviors.

1. Aggression: Boys are taught to be more aggressive than girls. They engage in more rough play and fighting, and are more often involved in violent and antisocial behavior.
2. Activity: Boys play outside more; they are encouraged to be more active and find it more difficult to sit still.

3. Curiosity: Boys are expected to be more curious—to explore and to find out how things work.
4. Impulsivity: Boys are expected to be more impulsive than girls—they have more trouble resisting temptation, become distracted more easily, and get into more dangerous situations. They take more chances than females.
5. Anxiety: Females are more fearful and anxious than males. Manifestations of anxiety are in compliant and obedient behaviors and in the showing of more interest in doing the right thing.
6. Importance of Social Relationships: Females are encouraged to be more nurturant from an early age. They show more interest in babies and play with dolls more. In more general terms, they display more empathy and show cooperation and compromise in social relationships.
7. Self-concept: Males are socialized to view themselves as more powerful and having more control over events—they can make a difference, and can make things happen.
8. Achievement-Related Behavior: Males expect to do better and set higher levels of aspiration for themselves. Females feel less confident and often doubt their abilities.

Dramatic characters (396 males and 75 females) were coded according to these eight sex-role attibutes by using a fairly simple judgment code: 0 = no evidence of the attribute in the relevant story, 1 = some, and 2 = much. Sex-role differences were tested by both chi-square tests, the t-test, and the Mann-Whitney "U" test, with significant differences being found between female and male characters on five of the eight scales and in the predicted directions (see Table 8.1). Males were found to show more aggression and activity and to score higher on self-concept and on achievement-related behaviors. Females evidenced greater concern with social relationships. In addition, although not reaching a high level of statistical significance, females demonstrated more anxiety. Male and female characters showed no overall significant differences in curiosity or impulsivity.

Although the general pattern of sex-role attributes held true for most major characters, there were some interesting differences or tendencies among female and male heroes and villains (see Table 8.2).* For example, although male heroes still tended to be more aggressive and active than female heroes, and female heroes were higher in concern for social relationships, they were roughly equal in self-concept and achievement-related behaviors. For villains, however, females tended to show higher levels of aggression and impulsivity, and exceeded males in

---

*Because of the small number of female hero and villain figures, high levels of statistical significance were not achieved in many cases. Predicted tendencies are also discussed here with this caveat in mind.

Table 8.1   Sex-Role Attributes, All Dramatic Characters

SEX-ROLE ATTRIBUTE	PERCENTS			MEAN SCORES		
	MALE	FEMALE	p	MALE	FEMALE	p
Aggression						
0 = none	34%	63%				
1 = some	37	21	(a)	0.95	0.53	(a)
2 = much	29	16				
Activity						
0 = none	15	25				
1 = some	44	45	(b)	1.27	1.04	(b)
2 = much	41	29				
Curiosity						
0 = none	72	67				
1 = some	24	24		0.33	0.43	
2 = much	4	9				
Impulsivity						
0 = none	76	75				
1 = some	20	24		0.28	0.27	
2 = much	4	1				
Anxiety						
0 = none	58	49				
1 = some	35	37	(d)	0.50	0.64	(d)
2 = much	7	13				
Social relationships						
0 = none	50	36				
1 = some	43	45	(a)	0.56	0.83	(a)
2 = much	7	19				
Self-concept						
0 = none	29	52				
1 = some	41	35	(a)	1.00	0.61	(a)
2 = much	30	13				
Achievement-related behavior						
0 = none	40	56				
1 = some	44	32	(b)	0.76	0.56	(b)
2 = much	16	12				

Note: For percentage distributions, significance was tested by chi-square; for differences between mean scores, the Mann-Whitney "U" test was employed. Probabilities are reported as follows: (a) indicates $p < .01$; (b) indicates $p < 0.5$; (c) indicates $p < .10$; (d) indicates $p < .20$. Mean scores are based on ratings of 0 = no evidence of an attribute; 1 = some evidence; 2 = much evidence. Thus, for the attribute of aggression, the male mean score of 0.95 is significantly higher than that for females (0.53). N = 396 males and 75 females.

Table 8.2 Sex-Role Attributes, by Dramatic Role and Sex

SEX-ROLE ATTRIBUTE	HEROES		VILLAINS		OTHER MAJOR ROLES	
	MALE	FEMALE	MALE	FEMALE	MALE	FEMALE
(N)	(94)	(13)	(82)	(6)	(220)	(56)
Aggression	1.06	0.69 (c)	1.61	1.83	0.65	0.36 (a)
Activity	1.62	1.38 (c)	1.18	1.00	1.15	0.96 (c)
Curiosity	0.44	0.69 (d)	0.12	0.00	0.36	0.41
Impulsivity	0.28	0.31	0.16	0.50 (b)	0.33	0.23
Anxiety	0.33	0.38	0.39	0.17	0.61	0.75 (d)
Social relationships	0.88	1.23 (c)	0.04	0.17 (d)	0.62	0.80 (c)
Self-concept	1.44	1.31	1.20	1.67 (d)	0.74	0.34 (a)
Achievement-related behavior	1.10	1.15	0.94	1.83 (a)	0.54	0.29 (a)

Note: Figures are mean scores for each sex-role attribute. Differences between each pair of scores were tested by using the Mann-Whitney "U" test. Probabilities are reported as follows: (a) indicates p < .01; (b) indicates p < .05; (c) indicates p < .10; (d) indicates p < .20.

58

self-concept and achievement-related behaviors. This could mean that females, in villain roles, are looked at as much more of a threat and display greater confidence in achieving what they set out to do. This conclusion is further supported in examining personality traits displayed by the characters.

PERSONALITY TRAITS

As a group, male characters are portrayed as stronger, more independent, and more active than females. Females, on the whole, were more serious, unselfish, good, peaceful, kind, intelligent, and warm than males. They were also shown as more passive, dependent, and weak than males. Physically, females were relatively thinner, more handsome, and better dressed than their male counterparts (see Table 8.3).

These portrayals were true for most major characters, and generally so for male and female hero characters. Female villains, however, were rated as stronger, more independent, and more active than their male counterparts (see Table 8.4).

Table 8.3 Personality Traits, by Sex

PERSONALITY TRAIT	MEAN SCORES	
	MALE	FEMALE
Serious-comic	3.3	2.9 (a)
Strong-weak	2.6	2.8 (b)
Unselfish-selfish	3.1	2.8 (a)
Good-bad	2.8	2.3 (a)
Peaceful-violent	3.3	2.7 (a)
Kind-cruel	3.2	2.7 (a)
Intelligent-stupid	2.8	2.5 (c)
Independent-dependent	2.5	2.8 (a)
Warm-cool	2.8	2.4 (a)
Honest-dishonest	3.2	3.1 (d)
Active-passive	1.9	2.3 (a)
Thin-fat	3.0	2.2 (a)
Handsome-ugly	3.1	2.5 (a)
Agile-clumsy	2.7	2.7
Well dressed-sloppy	2.7	2.4 (a)

Note: For each set of adjectives, characters are rated on a five-point scale, with 1 representing the left-hand adjective and 5 the right-hand one. The Mann-Whitney "U" test of differences between male and female means as utilized, and probabilities are reported as follows: (a) indicates $p < .01$; (b) indicates $p < .05$; (c) indicates $p < .10$; (d) indicates $p < .20$.

Table 8.4 Personality Traits, by Dramatic Role and Sex

PERSONALITY TRAIT	HEROES		VILLAINS		OTHER MAJOR ROLES	
	MALE	FEMALE	MALE	FEMALE	MALE	FEMALE
(N)	(94)	(13)	(82)	(6)	(220)	(56)
Serious-comic	3.1	2.7 (d)	3.2	2.2 (a)	3.4	3.0 (a)
Strong-weak	2.0	2.4 (d)	2.6	2.0 (b)	2.8	2.9 (d)
Unselfish-selfish	2.4	2.3	4.1	4.3	3.0	2.7 (a)
Good-bad	1.9	1.8	4.3	4.2	2.7	2.2 (a)
Peaceful-violent	3.4	2.8 (b)	4.2	4.3	3.0	2.5 (a)
Kind-cruel	2.6	2.5	4.2	4.2	3.0	2.6 (a)
Intelligent-stupid	2.4	1.8 (b)	2.9	1.8 (a)	2.9	2.8
Independent-dependent	2.3	2.2	2.1	1.8	2.7	3.0 (b)
Warm-cool	2.5	2.5	3.6	3.5	2.6	2.2 (a)
Honest-dishonest	2.9	2.8	3.9	4.0	3.1	3.0
Active-passive	1.5	1.6	2.0	1.8	2.1	2.4 (b)
Thin-fat	2.8	2.0 (a)	3.3	2.5 (b)	3.1	2.3 (a)
Handsome-ugly	2.8	2.0 (a)	3.6	2.2 (a)	3.0	2.6 (a)
Agile-clumsy	2.3	2.2	2.9	2.8	2.8	2.8
Well dressed-sloppy	2.5	2.2 (d)	2.8	2.2 (b)	2.7	2.4 (a)

Note: Characters are rated on a five-point scale with 1 representing the left-hand adjective and 5 the right. Differences between pairs were tested by using Mann-Whitney "U" test, and probabilities are reported as follows: (a) indicates p < .01; (b) indicates p < .05; (c) indicates p < .10; (d) indicates p < .20.

Summary

Children's TV tends to reinforce traditional sex-role behaviors and personality traits extant in society. Thus, females are portrayed as being more passive in behavior and paying more attention to social relationships. They rate lower in aggression, and in self-concept and achievement-related behaviors—i.e., they seem less confident. They also display the virtues of unselfishness, kindness, and warmth, while being weaker, more peaceful, more dependent and more passive than males.

These conclusions hold true for most females. The exceptions are female heroes, who, except for strength and violent behaviors, show greater equality with males in activity and independence. Also, female villains tend to be rated as stronger, more intelligent and more independent than male villains. It is suggested that such portrayals may indicate that females, when put in negative power positions, seem to reflect a threat greater than that of males in similar roles. However, both female heroes and villains were rarely found. Out of 471 major dramatic characters, there were only 13 female heroes and six female villains.

Physically, females are rated as thinner, more handsome, and better dressed than males, whether portraying heroes, villains, or other major characters.

9 SUMMARY: PORTRAYALS OF SEX ROLES AND BEHAVIORS

Perhaps the most significant finding of this study of sex-role portrayals on children's television lies in the overwhelming proportion of male characters found. This lack of recognition of females is clearly evident in the summary data:

- 243 females represent 22 percent of 1,107 characters identified by sex
- 203 females represent 27 percent of 758 human characters
- 23 females represent 9 percent of 244 animal characters

There were also interesting demographic differences between female and male characters. Although greatly outnumbered in almost all demographic groups, females were cast as younger than males:

- 43 percent of teenage characters were female
- 31 percent of young adults were female
- 15 percent of middle-aged characters were female

Females were also more apt to have their marital status clearly defined and to be identified in family roles:

- 40 percent of single adults were female
- 45 percent of married adults were female
- 38 percent of all characters in family roles were female
- 17 percent of all characters not identified in family roles were female

They were more likely to appear in nonanimated comedy and drama than in cartoon comedy or in action/adventure drama:

- 31 percent of nonanimated-comedy and other drama characters were female
- 20 percent of animated cartoon-comedy characters were female
- 19 percent of action/adventure drama characters were female

Further, females were not well represented in important dramatic roles:

- 12 percent of dramatic heroes were female
- 7 percent of dramatic villains were female
- 16 percent of all major dramatic characters were female
- 27 percent of all minor dramatic characters were female

They were less often shown as employed, and when employed, were shown as professional entertainers, and clerical or household workers:

- 29 percent of females were employed
- 42 percent of males were employed
- 24 percent of professional and technical workers were female
- 50 percent of clerical workers were female
- 35 percent of household workers were female
- 12 percent of managerial and sales workers were female

Females were almost completely unrepresented in other occupation groups, such as craftsmen, operatives, transportation workers, laborers, farmers, and service workers.

In spite of their small numbers, female characters tended to uphold traditional values. They more often sought altruistic goals such as respect for others and devotion to the group, home, and family. When seeking self-goals, they more often were concerned with safety and self-preservation or power. Males, on the other hand, were more apt to engage in self-indulgence; seek wealth, fame, and thrills; and act out of hatred. Males also valued work and patriotism more than females did.

In attempting to achieve their goals, females relied on personal charm and dependence on others to a much greater extent than did males, who used violence, trickery or deceit, and persuasion.

Females are also portrayed in traditional sex-role patterns. They were found to be significantly less aggressive and active than males, had lower self-concepts, and rated lower on achievement-related behaviors. They demonstrated much greater concern for social relationships and exhibited slightly greater anxiety.

Traditional personality characteristics were also demonstrated by female and male characters. Males were seen as having more violent, strong, cruel, active, and independent personalities; whereas, females were unselfish, kinder, and warmer. Females were, however, more dependent and passive.

There is, in the several measures used in this study, strong and consistent evidence not only of a lack of recognition of female characters— through their sheer lack of numbers—but also of a lack of respect illustrated by the small proportions of females in roles of status and prestige in society. However, they do uphold many values of society that have been traditionally considered the province of the female—home and family values.

Perhaps we should not be surprised at these findings, for they tend to confirm a number of previous studies of sex-role stereotyping on television (see Chapter 4). What is difficult to understand is why television specifically designed for the child audience continues to be more extreme in its portrayals than that for adults. Whereas the research has indicated that there has been a leveling off of the male-to-female ratio in prime-time TV at about 2:1, this analysis shows children's TV at about 4:1—and, in some important roles, an even wider disparity.

Although one can find some examples of female superhero models in the TV programs for children, we have found the overall representations of males and females to be quite traditional and stereotyped. Moreover, in spite of the efforts by many groups to improve the status of women in society, and the efforts to influence the portrayals of the sexes on television, the research over the past decade has shown that they are not changing in children's programs.

As a representation of some of the real changes taking place in the status of women in society, children's television provides a distorted mirror, with outdated models for young children. At this time, commercial children's television programs represent part of a pattern of persistent barriers to social change.

III
Portrayals of Minorities

10 MINORITIES AND TELEVISION

This chapter presents a review of previous research that illustrates the important role television plays in teaching children about other racial and ethnic groups, and its function in providing models of behaviors, values, and attitudes, and in mediating the self-esteem of children of minority racial and ethnic groups (Clark, 1969, 1972). Also included in this chapter is a review of recent research reports examining portrayals of minorities in fictional television presentations.

Television provides for millions of American children (and adults) the only extended contact that they have with members of different racial and ethnic groups (Atkin, Greenberg, and McDermott, 1977). As it entertains, TV also serves as a window on the world of those who are different. What life is like on TV provides children with a complex portrait of societal customs, values, morals, and expectations. How various people are portrayed can affect children's perceptions of certain kinds of men and women, and boys and girls. Media images become even more important when the child does indeed identify with a character. Positive portrayals that the child can identify with will enhance the child's concept about the character as well as about him or herself. Likewise, a negative portrayal may affect a child adversely, as noted by Jeffries (1979, p. 116):

> Media images can be important, first because one's self-image has been shown to be greatly determined by evaluations received from other sources including media. According to Jones' self-esteem theory, a person will respond favorably to a positive evaluation which satisfies self-esteem needs and will respond unfavorably to a negative evaluation.

Clark (1972) pointed out that the media in the United States were in part responsible for lowering blacks' self-esteem. Therefore, it seems imperative that we investigate how minorities are being shown in the world of children's television. If young people are to grow up with positive reinforcement and meaningful interpretations about people of all races and ethnic groups, the current media messages should not be a hindrance to this process.

OBSERVATIONAL LEARNING

Although children learn in a variety of ways, most social scientists agree that young people learn a great deal by imitating models provided in their environment (Bandura, 1969; Mischel, 1966). This process of observational learning occurs when a child watches television. Thus, along with other cultural and biological factors, TV portrayals offer children the opportunity to learn social behaviors from role models involved in real or fictional circumstances.

Often, fictional and fantasy TV shows that children watch make heavy use of formula plots and convenient stereotypes (Cantor, 1980). The initial role models that children see on TV could be puppets, animated characters, or human beings—all will serve to implant distinct messages, about societal values, ideas, and behaviors, in the mind of the child. These early observational models for children also create a foundation for future learning.

Because of their limited experiences and lack of cognitive sophistication, young children often cannot distinguish between fantasy and reality in television presentations, and hence are vulnerable to absorbing distorted, undesired, and uninterested messages from television presentations. Heavy TV viewers are at even greater risk of becoming dependent on TV as a source of information about how to conduct their interactions in everyday life.

Stereotypes and Consequences for Young Viewers

Since the word "stereotype" came into use about 60 years ago, many people have been in disagreement over its definitions and connotations. Brigham (1971) has implied that theorists remain divided over the relationship of ethnic stereotypes to negative attitudes and discriminatory behavior, but he states that most social scientists have regarded stereotypes as wrong either because they do not correspond to the facts about an ethnic group, or because they were arrived at through some unacceptable process. Stereotypes enable people to conveniently categorize and consequently make judgments about another person or group. But a stereotype differs from an ordinary generalization. Klineberg (1951, p. 505, reviewed in Brigham [1971, p. 18]) describes the distinguishing features of a stereotype:

> Unlike other generalizations, . . . stereotypes are based not on an inductive collection of data, but on hearsay, rumor, and anecdotes—in short, on evidence which is insufficient to justify the generalization.

Most of the research concerning minority stereotypes in the media has focused on the portrayal of blacks. Becker (1974) found that programs aimed at young children and that show black characters tend to provide stereotypes, rather than multidimensional portrayals. Atkin, Greenberg, and McDermott (1977) have outlined some of the ideas in the minds of white viewers that are affected by stereotyped TV blacks: beliefs about traits associated with black people; beliefs about dissimilarities between the attributes of white and black people; beliefs about the incidence of blacks in various segments of the population; and subjective general knowledge about blacks.

Atkin, Greenberg, and McDermott (1977) reported that substantial proportions of both black and white youths in California and Michigan samples cited TV as a major source of information about the world and, in particular, information about job roles and behavior patterns. Approximately two-fifths of their sample of nearly 1,000 white children reported TV as their main source of information about black people. Results also indicated that for white children, the importance of TV as a source increased as direct contact with blacks decreased. For example, about 68 percent of the rural white children reported TV as a major source of information about "how black people talk, look, and dress," as compared with only 20 percent of the urban white children reporting TV as a primary source of information about blacks.

The stereotypical presentations of minority characters on television may have special significance to minority youngsters. Numerous studies conducted during the last 15 years consistently indicate that blacks watch more television than do whites (Allen, 1981; Comstock, 1979; Bogart, 1972; Greenberg and Atkin, 1978; Bower, 1973). Furthermore, blacks, to a greater extent than whites, report using the media as sources of information about the world and view TV as a reliable source to a greater extent than do whites (Comstock and Cobbey, 1979; Allen and Bielby, 1979; Allen, 1981). For example, Atkin, Greenberg, and McDermott (1977) report that, in their sample of black and white youths from Michigan and California, black youths spent more time watching TV programs than white youths; were more accepting of television messages, perceiving that TV fictional portrayals accurately reflect real life; were more likely than whites to report TV as a source of useful information about social behavior and of occupational information; reported learning more about black people from TV (than did white youths); perceived black TV performers as possessing more positive traits than white characters; and identified more closely with television characters, seeking them as models.

Hartmann and Husband (1974, reviewed in Murray [1980, p. 46]) who interviewed people from areas with small and large immigrant populations, demonstrated how the media define or help to define the audience member's view of race relations. They found that those people who came in contact with immigrants often were more likely to rely on their own experience rather than on perceptions provided by the media. Ashmore and McConahay (1975) also drew conclusions about presentations of minority groups on television. They suggested that the manner in which ideas and attitudes about specific minorities were emphasized (or omitted) caused viewers to develop correspondingly biased perspectives about those groups. Noble drew conclusions similar to those drawn from the Atkin et al. study cited above. He concluded (1975, reviewed in Murray [1980, p. 46]):

> . . . children's perceptions of occupational roles and ethnic stereo-
> types are related to the secondhand or vicarious experiences on televi-
> sion. To the extent that the child lacks any countervailing personal
> experience, the more vulnerable he or she is to the televised reality.
> Other studies conducted with English school children have confirmed
> the notion that the television world is most powerful when the child
> does not have firsthand experiences of the reality in question.

In summary, results of numerous studies indicate that, due to stereotyping in television content, it is probable that children draw assumptions about minority groups from a limited range of images. Their attitudes and behaviors will, in turn, reflect the stereotypes they have been exposed to.

THE EVOLUTION OF MINORITIES ON TV

Clark (1969) described the presentation of minority groups on television as a selection process that passes through four stages: nonrecognition, ridicule, regulation, and respect. In brief, Clark described the stages as follows. Nonrecognition refers to scarce representation of a minority group, considered a kind of exclusion in a mass medium of communication. Ridicule takes into account groups that were formerly nonrecognized, but at the expense of making fun of them. It has two functions: the group that is being laughed at feels that ridicule is better than being ignored; and members of the dominant segment of society feel a boost to their self-esteem by ridiculing the other group. Regulation occurs in response to the cultural images created by the mass media when an oppressed group reacts, through pressure-group protests or vi-

bellion, and lashes out at the negative representation it has ex-
...d. Respect comes in the form of acceptable recognition of a
...ortrayed in a natural fashion by the mass media.

...m recognition to eventual respect, Clark's measure of minorities
...ass media is applicable to all races and ethnic groups. His frame-
...useful for examining the portrayal of minorities.

...or to 1965, few minorities appeared on TV at all. Until 1968,
...inority groups continued to be excluded from the medium, most
...the black, Mexican, or American Indian minorities. However, by
...of 1969, the number of minority portrayals had increased (Seg-
...Wheeler, 1973).

...il rights as an issue related to television's portrayal of minorities
was investigated by the Kerner Commission in its 1968 *Report of the
National Advisory Commission on Civil Disorders* (reviewed in U.S. Commission on Civil Rights [1977, pp. 1–2]). Mainly concerned with the portrayal of blacks in the media, the commission found that their visibility
was low and that when blacks were seen, they were shown from the
viewpoint of white people. This indictment of the media can be pro-
jected to other racial and ethnic minorities such as native Americans,
Asian-Americans, and people of Spanish origin, who continue to remain
scarce on television programs.

Near the end of the 1960s, appeals for minority rights did create an
increase in their number on television, particularly for blacks. However,
the variety of roles assigned to blacks has remained limited (Donagher,
Poulos, Liebert, and Davidson, 1975), and the most recent evidence
reveals a trend toward continued stability at about the 10-percent
level—i.e., for the past decade, the numbers of black characters in relation to white characters on television has remained at about 10 percent
(Greenberg, 1980). A 1981 study published by Seggar et al. shows that
this trend may even be reversing itself, as demonstrated by a decline in
the proportional representation of minorities in drama and comedy
programs.

Minority Portrayals on TV Programs

Given the evidence, cited above, that children use television as an
important source of information about people who belong to minority
racial and ethnic groups with whom they have limited contact, it is important to examine the portrayals of minority groups on television. This
section presents a summary of the results of content analyses of portrayals of minorities in fictional television presentations during the last
two decades.

In general, the results of these studies indicate that "members of
racial and ethnic minority groups are underrepresented in relation to

their numbers in the general population, and that they are portrayed in narrow, traditional and/or stereotypical ways" (Signorielli, 1981). Furthermore, during the last 25 years the situation has not changed, except that slightly more blacks have been included in fictional television presentations in the late 1960s and early 1970s.

Gerbner and Signorielli (1979) reported the results of a content analysis of characters populating prime-time and network weekend-daytime drama programs and of some viewer conceptions associated with exposure to television. The analysis is based on ten years (1969–78) of monitoring 1,365 programs and analyzing 16,888 characters.

Results of their long-term analysis indicate that television drama presents a world in which men outnumber women three to one; blacks and Hispanics are underrepresented; most majority types get proportionally more leading roles than do minority types; weekend-daytime children's programs both conceal and exaggerate the inequalities reflected in prime time.

Total female representation changed little, if at all, between 1969 and 1978, and the increase in the percentage of female leads was mostly for whites; there was no corresponding increase in the percentage of nonwhite female leads.

The percentage of all nonwhite characters increased very slowly and in small increments through 1977 and then dropped in 1978. The increase was limited, on the whole, to minor characters. Major nonwhite characters fluctuated between 4 and 13 percent of the prime-time population through 1977 and in 1978 accounted for 5 percent. During the same time period, nonwhite female leads ranged between 1 and 4 percent of the prime-time population; in 1978 they accounted for only 1 percent.

Overall, Gerbner and Signorielli found that the "slow and slight increase in the proportion of minor nonwhites is largely due to the rise in the percent of blacks since 1971 (until 1978). Major Hispanic and Oriental characters became visible in the early 1970s, maintained a steady but miniscule presence through the mid-70s, and have declined since then through 1976." The same trends discussed above were found in children's daytime programming, but these trends could not be reliably analyzed on an annual basis because of the small numbers of characters in minority categories.

An in-depth analysis of the data available for 1973 and 1974 from the Annenberg Cultural Indicators Research Project (U.S. Commission on Civil Rights, 1977) further illuminates the portrayals of racially and ethnically identified nonwhite characters. In 1973 they found 109 nonwhite characters identifiable by racial or ethnic origin; in 1974 they found 115.

Black males constituted over or nearly one-half of all minority characters (54.1 percent in 1973 and 41.6 percent in 1974), followed by Asian-Americans (18.4 percent in 1973 and 19.1 percent in 1974), and black females (13.8 percent in 1973 and 18.3 percent in 1974). Asian-American female characters and Hispanic and native-American characters of both sexes constituted the remainder. Four out of five minority characters were males. Nonwhite characters appeared in over half of the programs aired in 1973 and 1974, but constituted only 12.2 percent and 12.5 percent of all characters, respectively.

Several patterns emerged regarding the types of programs on which nonwhites appeared, and the ways in which they were depicted. Over two-thirds of the action/adventure programs included at least one nonwhite character and nearly one-half of the nonwhite characters appeared on action/adventure shows. In several series of this type, groups of minority characters were all involved in the same activity. For example, in one episode of "Kung Fu," 11 Asian-American characters were affiliated with a religious order; an episode of "Hawaii Five-O" featured a ring of Hawaiian gangsters; and ten African tribesmen accounted for the portrayals of most nonwhite characters on the program "Born Free" (U.S. Commission on Civil Rights, 1977, p. 38). Nonwhite characters also appeared on many action/adventure series in token roles as service workers, doctors, and police officers.

Situation comedies set in foreign or ethnic locales—Korea, the black ghetto, or the barrio—were the only ones with more than token appearances of nonwhite characters. With one exception (a series featuring an integrated high school), nonwhites had only token roles. (To be counted as a token, a nonwhite character had to be the only minority individual on the episode being coded. No nonwhite character coded as a token played a leading role.)

Finally, fewer than half of the nonwhite minor female characters (13 out of 35) in the two-year period analyzed were legally and gainfully employed, and their occupations were largely stereotyped and subordinate, i.e., nurses, secretaries, receptionists, maids, and a cook. Black-female minor characters were cast most frequently as prostitutes (U.S. Commission on Civil Rights, 1977, p. 40).

Seggar and Wheeler (1973) analyzed the portrayal of minorities on TV in 1971 in order to assess the extent to which major minorities were represented, and to compare their portrayals with white-American portrayals. Sampling 250 half-hour units, during five consecutive weeks in February and March of 1971, they made observations of 1,830 portrayals. Data collected related to occupational roles, sex, ethnicity, and duration of the performance. Portrayals represented white Americans, and minority groups including American Indians, Armenians, Australians, black Americans, Brazilians, Cubans, the Chinese, the Dutch, East

Europeans, the English, the French, Germans, Greeks, Hawaiians, Hungarians, the Irish, Italians, the Japanese, Latin Americans, Mexicans, Orientals, Russians, Scots, and the Spanish.

Their findings were consistent with major findings of other content analyses. That is, minority groups were severely underrepresented in comparison with census data on their actual numbers in the United States. There was also a trend in the sampled portrayals for professional, technical, and service categories to be overrepresented for all ethnic groups. Examination of a rank ordering of the five most frequently aired occupations for each group indicated that black and Chicano males each had over 50 percent of their portrayals in five occupations, most of which were service occupations, in contrast to 29.1 percent of all white American males, who were shown as physicians, policemen, musicians, servicemen, and government diplomats. Over half of every group of females was shown in five occupations, indicating serious limitations on the roles available to women.

Finally, an examination of the length of portrayals indicated that the larger percentages of minority-group members were found in performances limited to under three minutes of air time (a figure which is correlated with minor roles). For example, while approximately 64 percent of white Americans and 65 percent of those classified as Europeans had roles limited to less than three minutes, 84 percent of the Chicanos (the term as used by Seggar and Wheeler includes all Hispanics) and 72 percent of all blacks, were similarly limited in the duration of their performances.

Hinton et. al. (1974) examined tokenism and stereotyping in the portrayals of blacks on 133 commercial network programs during six weeks in February and March of 1973. They gathered information on 317 different portrayals, of which 168 (53 percent) were of whites and 149 (47 percent) were of blacks, representing a ratio of ten whites to one black on network television.

They found that only eight of the 133 programs sampled featured a black actor or actress as a regular. In five of these shows the featured black shared the lead with several whites. Blacks were shown significantly more often than whites in bit parts and minor roles. In their sample of programs, no black female was cast in a major role, and only twice was a black female featured in a supporting role.

Six stereotypes were selected for analysis: industriousness, competence, attractiveness, hostility, morality, dominance. For each trait, it was hypothesized that blacks would be portrayed more negatively than whites. The data did not support these hypotheses. Blacks were not shown significantly more often than whites as lazy, incompetent, and unattractive; and whites were portrayed more often than blacks as hostile and violent, and were more often portrayed in immoral and illegal roles than blacks.

Dominance was the only category in which black portrayals were less favorable than white portrayals. Blacks were portrayed as subordinate 11 percent more often than they were portrayed as dominant, which could be construed as negative stereotyping. Overall, the results of this study indicated that blacks, and, in particular, black males, were generally portrayed as industrious, competent, and law-abiding in the few roles open to them, but that they were still relegated to minor and insignificant roles.

Seggar, Hafen, and Hannonen-Gladden (1981) conducted a followup study to their earlier studies, which examined representation of minorities in fictional media presentations. The goals of this study were to determine whether there was evidence to show that gains made by minorities up to 1971 had been maintained during the 1970s; to determine the trends for women; and to determine whether changes occurred in the role significance of minorities and women between 1975 and 1980. The four time periods sampled were five-week periods in February and March of 1971, 1973, 1975, and 1980.

Their examination of trends over the ten-year period under consideration indicated an increase in white domination of comedy-drama and drama shows; a maintaining of blacks' representation at about 6-to-8 percent; and a virtual exclusion of other minorities, who together accounted for less than 3 percent of the characters in fictional television presentations, despite the fact that collectively they comprised between 8 and 9 percent of the national population in 1978.

Throughout the ten-year period, females continued to be seriously underrepresented in comparison with males, despite increasing their representation slowly throughout the decade; female representation increased from 21 percent in 1971 to 39 percent in 1980.

Minority females were the most seriously underrepresented group in the fictional world of television. During the period of the analysis, black and other minority females consistently comprised fewer than 10 percent of the female population on television drama and comedy shows.

Finally, their results indicated that between 1975 and 1980, only white males and females increased their percentages of participation in major roles (as contrasted with supporting roles and bit parts). The percentage of black males in major roles dropped from 9.0 percent (of 233 major male roles) in 1975 to 4.4 percent (of 203 major male roles) in 1980; and the percentages of black females in major roles declined from 9.6 percent (of 83 major female roles) in 1975 to 2.4 percent (of 126 major female roles) in 1980. Other minority males actually increased their participation in major roles slightly (from 7.7 percent in 1975 to 8.4 percent in 1980). Other minority females continued their trend toward becoming nonexistent in television drama and comedy; their representation in major roles dropped from 3.6 percent of 83 major female roles in 1975 to 1.6 percent of 126 major female roles in 1980.

Finally, results of two studies in a recent series of reports on content analyses of U.S. TV drama between 1975 and 1978 describe the limited kinds of portrayals of black and Hispanic Americans to which American viewers are exposed.

Seeking to provide a comprehensive description of fictional television portrayals of Hispanic Americans, Greenberg and Baptista-Fernandez (1980) analyzed one sample week of programming from each of three seasons of commercial fictional programming (1975–76, 1976–77, and 1977–78). In a population of 3,549 they reliably identified 53 as Hispanic. (These 53 constituted less than 1.5 percent of the speaking TV characters). They found that Hispanic characters were unlikely to be continuing members of the cast of a series and were unlikely to be seen in more than one season of a show; Hispanics were most likely to be featured in episodes, centered around illegal aliens and criminal elements, that wouldn't reoccur.

Hispanic portrayals were dominated by Mexican-Americans and Puerto Ricans, and were predominantly of males (44 out of 53). The most common vocation was that of the crook, followed by the police officer. The remaining legal occupations held by Hispanic Americans included low-status service occupations (e.g., doorman, waiter, car-wash attendant, and handyman), and a few professional and technical occupations (including animal trainer, building inspector, and fireman).

Baptista-Fernandez and Greenberg (1980) also conducted an in-depth examination of the context, characteristics, and communication behaviors of blacks on television. Their study was based on a sample week of prime-time and Saturday-morning fictional series taped during the fall 1977 season. Sports, news, specials, variety shows, and movies were omitted from the sample. Forty-three of the 81 episodes taped had one or more black speaking characters. In all, 101 black characters and 484 white characters had speaking parts. Each episode was coded for characters' physical attributes (e.g., age, sex, occupation, socio-economic status, physique, and clothing style); for roles (good or bad person, and serious or comic role); for context variables of shows (e.g., duration; time of day; orginating network; program type—comedy, crime, cartoon, etc.; and racial composition of the show); and for social-interaction attributes (e.g., the ethnicity of each participant, and topics of conversation—sex, love, courtship, domestic matters, crime, business, etc.).

Briefly, they found that in comparison to whites, blacks tended to be "younger, leaner, flashier dressers," and more likely to appear in comedies. Blacks were also more likely than whites to be concentrated in the lowest socioeconomic levels and to be unemployed. Further, blacks were more likely to be cast either as the only black in a series, or as part of an extensive group of blacks. For example, six of the 41 shows including blacks contained 41 percent of all the black characters identified in the sample week. These six series were all black shows featuring black major characters ("Fat Albert," "Good Times," "Mohammed Ali," "Sanford Arms," "The Jeffersons," and "What's Happening!").

Minorities and Children's TV

The major research on the portrayal of minorities in programs designed specifically for children has been conducted for Action for Children's Television (ACT). Mendelson's and Young's 1972 study found (p. 2) at the beginning of the 1970s:

1. Black and other minority characters make up a small percentage of characters, 7 percent and 2 percent, respectively.
2. Over 60 percent of the shows with human characters have no black or minority characters at all; no show has only black or other minority characters.
3. Blacks and other minorities rarely appear in work situations, while whites often appear as managers, professionals, law officers, workers, and bums.
4. Blacks who are major characters are depicted generally with positive attributes, while whites are shown with both positive and negative traits.
5. There are several black heroes, but no black villains.
6. The occasional black leader has a white coleader, while most shows have white leaders.
7. Non-American and nonwhite cultures are referred to negatively almost four out of five times when they are mentioned.
8. Native Americans and Asians are almost always treated as negative stereotypes.
9. Only occasionally does a good character speak with an accent, or in a dialect, while over half the villains speak with accents, most commonly German or Russian ones.
10. Most shows have no interaction between races, and in most cases where there are integrated groups, there is one black among the group.
11. In the two shows with black stars, blacks interact only with white characters.
12. Race is never mentioned or discussed.

I examined samples of children's TV programs on commercial stations during the 1970s and revealed findings consistent with those of Mendelson and Young (see Barcus [1975a, 1975b, 1977, 1978a, 1978b]).

In five separate samples of programming, blacks never exceeded 7 percent of the population of human characters. Table 10.1 compares these different samples of programs, as well as figures related to commercial advertising and noncommercial, public-service announcements (PSAs).

Whites, blacks, and other minorities appear in similar proportions in commercial advertising messages, with blacks comprising from 5 to 8 percent of the characters involved. Other minorities have been even less represented in advertising, however, and comprise 2 percent or less of the characters in all the samples.

Spokespersons in commercials, however, were almost always white, with no black spokespersons showing up in any of three 1978 samples of ads, and with only a few other minorities in spokesperson roles. In all of children's television, minorities (especially blacks) seem most likely to appear in noncommercial, public-service announcements; in 1975 and 1977 samples of children's programs, they comprised from 10 percent to 23 percent of PSA characters.

In addition to the simple distributions cited in Table 10.1, which show a consistent underrepresentation of blacks and other minority characters in program and advertising matter, the ACT studies during the 1970s also showed consistent patterns in age distributions of minorities, and in the types of programs in which they were most likely to appear. Blacks, for example, are apt to be seen as child characters more frequently than as teens or adults. On 1975 weekend programs, 13 percent of all child characters were black; on 1977 weekend programs, 16 percent were black children. This compares to the overall percentage of 7 percent for all black characters.

The studies also showed that black and other minority characters were much more likely to be found in comedy dramas than in action/ adventure dramas, and also were more frequently represented in informational-type programs.

Summary

There is no doubt that recognition by television legitimizes the status of a particular individual or group in society. A group that is covered in the media is one that has arrived. In this sense, minorities have not yet arrived; they are still waiting for recognition by television. For a short while during the early 1970s, there was an increase in the number of minority characters on the television screen. Since then their numbers have seemed to stabilize and, for some groups, have diminished.

On children's television, minorities have appeared, but their numbers are still relatively scarce, and the trends illustrated by various studies reveal that over the 1970s, minorities did not gain strength in

Table 10.1 Percent of White, Black, and Other Minority Characters in Programs and Advertising, 1972–78

YEAR/SAMPLE	PERCENT WHITE	PERCENT BLACK	PERCENT OTHER MINORITIES	NUMBER OF CHARACTERS ANALYZED
Characters in Programs				
1972—weekend programming	91	7	2	(440)
1975—weekend programming	89	7	4	(288)
1975—weekday programming	96	3	1	(282)
1977—weekend programming	85	7	8	(332)
1977—weekday programming	93	3	4	(343)
Characters in commercial announcements				
1975—weekend program sample	92	8	—*	(1,157)
1975—weekday program sample	95	5	—*	(1,287)
1977—weekend program sample	90	8	2	(1,119)
1977—weekday program sample	92	6	2	(1,493)
Spokespersons in commercial announcements				
1975—weekend program sample	97	—	3	(72)
1977—weekday program sample	99	—	1	(135)
1978—sample of food advertising	98	—	2	(52)
Characters in noncommercial announcements (PSAs)				
1975—weekend program sample	84	11	5	(202)
1975—weekday program sample	72	23	5	(117)
1977—weekend program sample	86	10	4	(218)
1977—weekday program sample	86	10	4	(138)

*Less than ½ of 1 percent (three out of 1,157 characters on weekend advertising; one out of 1,287 characters on weekdays).
Sources: Mendelson and Young (1972); Barcus (1975a, 1975b, 1977, 1978a, 1978b).

relative proportions. The patterns in other areas of television correspond with the data observed in children's TV: that blacks may have made the most headway in terms of recognition, but this is still not reflective of their numbers in our society. Other minorities seem not to have fared even as well as blacks, since their numbers are barely noticeable.

There is sufficient evidence that children do learn about other ethnic groups from television, that characterizations of minority figures are often presented in stereotyped ways, and that information about minority groups may be gained especially by those who have limited direct experience with minorities. All of this suggests that special care should be taken in depicting subgroups of the population that are not dominant in our society.

More than a decade of research has consistently revealed patterns that indicate a lack of recognition and respect for minorities on television. The research has also indicated that children's television has even lower overall representations of minorities than does adult TV. It seems indeed odd that children, the segment of the population most in need of accurate portrayals, may be getting the least accurate information.

It is to a further investigation of these racial and ethnic portrayals in children's television that the next chapters are devoted.

11 RECOGNITION OF RACE AND ETHNICITY

In Chapter 5, the analysis of character compositions on children's programs revealed a somewhat segregated white world, with a majority of the program segments being composed of only white characters. This chapter is devoted to exploring the population distributions of white, black, and other minorities, as well as other ethnically identified characters. Up to ten characters were classified for each program segment. Major, submajor, and minor characters were all included if they had a speaking role in the segment; excluded were characters used in crowd scenes or in background settings.

In attempting to define race and ethnicity, we are dealing with a number of possible indicators such as skin color, national origin, geographical distributions, citizenship, and genetically transmitted physical characteristics. If cultural anthropologists, ethnologists, and geneticists often find difficulties in defining racial and ethnic origins, I will not attempt to provide a final solution to these difficulties here. However, it is necessary to provide the reader with a set of operational definitions so that further references in this book are not confusing.

In this study two terms are used to distinguish minority and other characters. The term "race" is used to refer only to human characters because it is not possible to identify animals and other nonhuman characters in children's television. The categories for race are roughly equivalent to the somewhat traditional classification of American minority groups. Tables using the category of race include the following groups:

1. white: characters not identified as defined below, but presumed to be majority Americans regardless of national origin;
2. black: based on skin color;
3. other minorities: Hispanics, Asians, native Americans, and Eskimos;

4. uncertain: nonwhites, but they are impossible to classify in the above categories; examples are alien human beings from another planet, cavemen, a mummy, a clown in makeup, and a blue-skinned character;
5. animals: not classified in terms of race; and
6. other nonhumans: robots or other anthropomorphic beings not classified.

A second set of classifications is described as "ethnicity." Unlike race, the ethnicity category allows classification of all characters (including animals or other nonhumans) if they were identified by surname, speech, dress, locale, language, accent, or national origin. A familiar example is Speedy Gonzales: Although classified as an animal character, he is clearly identified as Mexican by surname, dress, and accent.

The category of ethnicity thus includes race but also includes others identified primarily by national origin other than an American one. The categories used and examples of characters who appeared in the sample are as follows:

1. blacks: black Africans and Afro-Americans;
2. Europeans: Dutch, English, German, French, Irish, Italian, Jewish, Russian, Slavic, and Swiss characters;
3. Arabs: Egyptians and other Middle Eastern people unidentified by country;
4. Asians: Japanese, Chinese, and Hawaiian people;
5. Hispanics: Cuban, Mexican, Puerto Rican, and unidentified Spanish speakers;
6. other ethnics: native Americans, Eskimos, Amazons, and South American Indians;
7. nonethnics: the term is used to represent all other human or animal characters with no cues to ethnicity as defined above (approximately 70 percent unidentified white humans and 30 percent animal and nonhuman characters).

DISTRIBUTIONS BY RACE

Of all 1,145 characters appearing in all program segments, 758 (66 percent) were human characters classified by race. The remainder were animal characters, robots, or other anthropomorphic beings.

Of the human characters, approximately 87 percent were white, 5 percent black, and 6 percent were other minorities (see Table 11.1).

There were no significant differences among racial groups with regard to sex distributions (see Table 11.2). In all cases more than two-thirds of the characters were male.

Age distributions of racial groupings show that black characters appear significantly more often in child, teen, and young-adult roles

Table 11.1   Distribution of Characters, by Race

RACE OF CHARACTER	NUMBER OF CHARACTERS	PERCENT OF ALL CHARACTERS	PERCENT OF HUMAN CHARACTERS
White	659	57.5	86.9
Black	41	3.6	5.4
Other minorities	47	4.1	6.2
Uncertain	11	1.0	1.5
Animals and other nonhumans	387	33.8	—
Total (percent)		100.0	100.0
Total (number)	1,145	(1,145)	(758)

Table 11.2   Distribution of Characters, by Race and Sex

RACE OF CHARACTER	PERCENT MALE	BASE NUMBER
White	72.2	(659)
Black	68.3	(41)
Other minorities	74.5	(47)
Uncertain	81.8	(11)
All human characters	72.3	(758)

than do either whites or other minorities (Table 11.3). There were no elderly blacks, although the highest proportions of the elderly were in the other-minorities group (five out of 47 characters).

Marital status of white and minority characters differed to some extent. Whereas about one out of ten white characters were clearly identified as married, somewhat fewer black characters were so identified, and nearly twice the proportion of other minority characters were married (see Table 11.4). To be classified as a single adult (children and teens were not coded), there had to be some clear indication that an unattached single individual was looking for a date or dating the opposite sex, or otherwise indicating single status. One out of ten white characters were so identified. There were no black singles, and only two out of 47 minority characters were single.

DISTRIBUTIONS BY ETHNICITY

In addition to a classification by racial identity, categories of ethnicity were used to further analyze the portrayals of ethnic origins of the characters. Indeed, 184 of the 1,145 characters (including some animal characters—e.g., Speedy Gonzales) were classifiable by ethnicity; others

Table 11.3   Distribution of Characters, by Race and Age

| | RACE | | |
AGE GROUP OF CHARACTER	WHITE	BLACK	OTHER MINORITIES
Children	10.9%	24.4%	17.0%
Teens	13.1	19.5	12.8
Young adults	37.9	41.5	31.9
Middle-aged persons	34.1	14.6	27.7
Elderly	4.0	—	10.6
Total (percent)	100.0	100.0	100.0
Total (number)	(649)	(41)	(47)

Table 11.4   Distribution of Characters, by Race and Marital Status

| | RACE | | |
MARITAL STATUS	WHITE	BLACK	OTHER MINORITIES
Single	10.3%	—	4.3%
Married	10.2	7.3%	19.1
Widowed/divorced	0.5	—	—
Not applicable			
(children, teens)	22.9	43.9	27.7
Uncertain	56.1	48.8	48.9
Total (percent)	100.0	100.0	100.0
Total (number)	(659)	(41)	(47)

Note: Although there were many characters who appeared as unattached adults in the program segments, fairly strict coding rules were established to identify marital status. This is the reason for the large number of uncertain classifications represented in the table.

had insufficient cues for reliable classification and could be presumed to be either nonethnic Americans, or animals or other nonhumans lacking ethnic identities.* Therefore, about 16 percent of all characters had some clear ethnic identification.

The tabulation of the ethnic identification of all characters is shown in Table 11.5. In frequency, the preferred ethnic groups are white Europeans (including Anglo-Saxons, Nordics, the French, Germans, Italians, Russians, Slavics, and Jews). These account for 42 percent of all ethnic portrayals, followed by blacks (black Africans or Afro-Americans—23 percent), Hispanics (19 percent), Arabs (7 percent), and Asians (5 per-

---

*Cues for ethnicity were accents, dress, and national origin, along with surnames; names alone were not considered enough evidence of ethnicity for classification purposes.

Table 11.5   Characters Identified by Ethnicity

ETHNIC IDENTIFICATION	NUMBER	PERCENT OF ALL CHARACTERS	PERCENT OF THOSE IDENTIFIED BY ETHNICITY
Blacks			
Black African	3	0.3	1.6
Afro-American	38	3.3	20.7
Other blacks	1	0.1	0.5
Total	42	3.7	22.8
Europeans			
Dutch	1	0.1	0.5
English	40	3.5	21.7
French	6	0.5	3.3
German	11	0.9	6.0
Irish	9	0.8	4.9
Italian	2	0.2	1.1
Jewish	2	0.2	1.1
Russian	1	0.1	0.5
Slavic	3	0.2	1.6
Swiss	2	0.2	1.1
Total	77	6.7	41.8
Arabs			
Egyptian	11	0.9	6.0
Other Arabs	2	0.2	1.1
Total	13	1.1	7.1
Asians			
Chinese	6	0.5	3.3
Hawaiian	1	0.1	0.5
Japanese	1	0.1	0.5
Other, unidentified	1	0.1	0.5
Total	9	0.8	4.9
Hispanics			
Cuban	7	0.6	3.8
Mexican	22	1.9	12.0
Puerto Rican	1	0.1	0.5
Other Spanish-speaking	5	0.4	2.7
Total	35	3.0	19.0
Other ethnics			
Native American	1	0.1	0.5
Amazon	2	0.2	1.1
Alien	3	0.2	1.6
Eskimo	1	0.1	0.5
South American Indian	1	0.1	0.5
Total	8	0.7	4.4
Total, ethnically identified	184	16.1	100.0
Not identified ethnically	961	83.9	
Total, all characters	1,145	100.0	

cent). Only one identifiable native American appeared among the 1,145 characters: Tonto of "The-Lone-Ranger" fame.

Since these distributions include all characters, regardless of the type of program in which they appear, they are looked at further by type of program in Table 11.6. This analysis demonstrates an interesting pattern whereby certain ethnic groups are more likely to appear in programs intended to provide information to the viewer, rather than being integrated into the plots of comedy or other dramatic presentations.

For example, whereas blacks comprise approximately 23 percent of all ethnically identified characters, they represent nearly 40 percent of those in informational-type programs but only 8 percent of those in comedy dramas. The same pattern is true for Hispanic and Asian characters but not for Arabs and Europeans, who were more often found in dramas.

Although male characters greatly outnumbered females in all ethnic groups, there was a higher proportion of female characters among blacks than among any other ethnic group. Whereas females comprised 22 percent of all characters, they amounted to 21 percent of all ethnics combined—only 15 percent of Arabs, 14 percent of Europeans, but 31 percent of blacks (see Table 11.7).

Blacks were also portrayed as significantly younger than other ethnic groups and all characters combined. There were proportionately more children, teens, and young adults among blacks than in other ethnic groups, whereas other ethnic characters were proportionately more often shown as middle-aged or elderly than were either blacks or nonethnic characters (see Table 11.8).

Table 11.6 Distribution of Ethnically Identified Characters, by Type of Program

ETHNIC GROUP	COMEDY DRAMAS[a]	ALL OTHER DRAMAS[b]	INFORMATIONAL PROGRAMS	ALL SEGMENTS
Blacks	8.3%	24.7%	39.5%	22.8%
Europeans	56.7	48.2	9.3	41.8
Arabs	8.3	9.9	—	7.1
Asians	5.0	3.7	7.0	4.9
Hispanics	20.0	4.9	44.2	19.0
Other ethnics	1.7	8.6	—	4.4
Total (percent)	100.0	100.0	100.0	100.0
Total (number)	(60)	(81)	(43)	(184)

[a]Primarily cartoon comedies.
[b]Mostly action/adventure dramas.

Table 11.7   Distribution of Ethnic Characters, by Sex

ETHNIC GROUP	MALE	FEMALE	PERCENT OF EACH GROUP WHO WERE MALE
Blacks	19.9%	34.2%	69
Europeans	45.2	28.9	86
Arabs	7.5	5.3	85
Asians	4.8	5.3	78
Hispanics	18.5	21.0	77
Other ethnics	4.1	5.3	75
Total (percent)	100.0	100.0	
Total (number)	(146)	(38)	79
Not ethnically identified	(718)	(205)	78

Table 11.8   Distribution of Ethnic Characters, by Age Group

AGE GROUP	BLACKS	ALL OTHER ETHNIC GROUPS	NOT IDENTIFIED ETHNICALLY
Children	23.8%	11.5%	15.0%
Teens	19.0	8.0	13.3
Young adults	42.9	29.2	36.9
Middle-aged persons	14.3	42.5	30.8
Elderly	—	8.8	4.0
Total (percent)	100.0	100.0	100.0
Total (number)	(42)	(113)	(646)

Summary

Whether looked at by the race or ethnicity categories, the analysis here has shown minorities to be considerably underrepresented in children's television when compared to their proportions in society. Blacks are portrayed as younger than whites, and other minorities tend to be older. In frequency, white foreigners are more often portrayed than are other ethnic groups. They are, however, not always treated with great respect, as will be seen in Chapter 12.

12 THE TREATMENT OF MINORITIES

As stated in the Introduction, content measures of respect are indicated by the treatment of various groups in the programs. One measure is in the assignment of various racial or ethnic groups to major or minor roles. Other measures include the social class and occupational roles of the characters.

HEROES, VILLAINS, AND OTHERS

Of all human characters, both black and white characters were equally likely to be cast as heroes, whereas other minorities were more frequently cast as villains in proportion to their numbers (see Table 12.1). Most villainous of all were nonhuman characters and those with uncertain racial identities. Other minority villains included, for example, a Spanish-speaking kidnapper, a blue-skinned evildoer, and a Puerto Rican clock thief.

Black hero figures included Superstretch and Microwoman, The Brown Hornet in a segment of the "New Fat Albert Show," and a black child in another segment. Blacks were also cast in proportionately greater numbers of major roles than were other human characters.

Compared with all ethnically identified characters, blacks were cast more frequently as major characters overall, and in hero roles, and less often as villains (see Table 12.2). Other ethnics are twice as likely to be assigned minor roles than are either blacks or other characters.

U.S. or foreign citizenship was reliably identified for most of the human characters. Both white and black characters were predominantly shown as U.S. citizens, whereas only slightly more than one-half of other minorities were (see Table 12.3).

Table 12.1 Race, by Dramatic Role

DRAMATIC ROLE	HUMAN CHARACTERS				NONHUMAN CHARACTERS		
	WHITE	BLACK	OTHER	UNCERTAIN	ANIMALS	NONHUMAN	TOTAL
Heroes	10.3%	9.8%	6.4%	9.1%	9.6%	7.8%	9.7%
Villains	6.4	2.4	8.5	18.2	10.0	16.4	8.3
Other major characters	31.1	41.5	34.0	36.4	40.9	26.7	33.5
Total, major characters	47.8	53.7	48.9	63.7	60.5	50.9	51.5
Submajor	28.7	31.7	27.7	27.3	20.7	31.0	27.1
Minor characters	23.5	14.6	23.4	9.1	18.8	18.1	21.4
Total, minor characters	52.2	46.3	51.1	36.4	39.5	49.1	48.5
All roles (percent)	100.0	100.0	100.0	100.0	100.0	100.0	100.0
All roles (number)	(659)	(41)	(47)	(11)	(271)	(116)	(1145)

Table 12.2   Ethnicity, by Dramatic Role

DRAMATIC ROLE	BLACK ETHNICS	ALL OTHER ETHNICS	NONETHNIC CHARACTERS*
Heroes	11.9%	2.1%	10.7%
Villains	2.4	8.4	8.5
Other major characters	40.5	26.8	34.2
Total, major characters	54.8	37.3	53.4
Submajor characters	30.9	26.8	27.0
Minor characters	14.3	35.9	19.6
Total, minor characters	45.2	62.7	46.6
Total (percent)	100.0	100.0	100.0
Total (number)	(42)	(142)	(961)

*Includes whites, animals, and others not identified by ethnicity.

Table 12.3   Race and Ethnicity, by Citizenship

CLASSIFICATION	PERCENT U.S. CITIZENS	TOTAL NUMBER CLASSIFIED*
Race		
White	91.1	463
Black	92.1	38
Other minorities	52.4	42
Ethnic Group		
Blacks	92.3	39
Other ethnics	31.5	89
Not identified ethnically	93.2	483

*Totals do not equal total of whites, blacks or others because some could not be identified as to citizenship.

Nonblack ethnically identified characters (categorized above as other ethnics) were most often of foreign citizenship. That is, when English, German, Asian, Arab, and other such groups were identified, the action most frequently took place in a foreign land and these groups assumed foreign-citizenship status.

SOCIAL CLASS AND OCCUPATIONAL STATUS OF MINORITIES

An initial indicator of social status is the extent to which different groups are depicted as employed individuals—that is, employed in legitimate money-earning occupations. Looking at human characters only, 50 percent were shown as being employed. A much smaller percentage of animal and other characters were shown as employed. However, white characters were much more likely to hold jobs than were minority characters (see Table 12.4); whereas more than one-half of whites were shown as employed, just over one-third of blacks and other minorities were so depicted.

Of those who were employed, however, more than one-half of both black and white characters held professional and managerial positions, whereas other minorities predominated as craftsmen and service workers. Other minorities were also more likely to be cast as housewives and in illegal occupations (see Table 12.5).

Majority and minority characters were also classified by social class, by utilizing occupation, standard of living, and other cues for classification. Other minorities here also were shown in lower-middle- and lower-class settings and occupations to a much greater extent than were either white or black characters (see Table 12.6).

Although these statistics provide a fairly consistent general picture of the treatment of minorities, they are also misleading to some extent. A closer look at the actual occupations and other roles reveals several stereotypes that prevail in the cartoons and other programs for children. Census categories of professionals, for example, include a variety of performers, sports professionals, and others. In addition, most of the minority professionals appear not in the general dramatic fare of children's TV, but in those programs that are designed to inform and orient the young child to realistic minority occupations. The nature of some of the minority and ethnic stereotypes can be seen by inspecting the list in Table 12.7 of ethnically identified roles as they appear in cartoon comedies, other dramatic programs, and informational programs.

With the exception of the characters in informational programs, minor-character portrayals were greatly stereotyped for ethnic subgroups. The following roles illustrate:

Black Roles	Asian Roles	Hispanic Roles
African diplomat	Cook	Bullfight announcer
African village laborer	Rickshaw man	Construction worker
Police chief	Busboy	Ship's cook
Musician	Dragon lady	Kidnapper
Mechanic		Cafe owner

Germanic	French	Other Roles
Surgeon	Cook/chef	Italian opera singer
Doctor	Spy	Indian river guide
Scientist		Irish cop
Music professor		English butler
Housekeeper		
Dutch ship's captain		

Table 12.4 Race and Ethnicity, by Employment Status

CLASSIFICATION	PERCENT EMPLOYED	TOTAL NUMBER
Race		
White	52.2	659
Black	36.6	41
Other minorities	34.0	47
Uncertain	36.4	11
Animal characters	13.3	271
Other nonhumans	19.8	116
Ethnic Group		
Blacks	38.1	42
Other ethnics	50.7	142
Not identified ethnically	36.4	961
Human characters only	50.0	758
All characters	38.3	1,145

Table 12.5 Race, by Occupation

OCCUPATION	WHITE	BLACK	OTHER MINORITIES
Professional and managerial	54.8%	57.8%	28.0%
Clerical and sales workers	3.0	—	—
Craftsmen and operatives	9.6	10.5	16.0
Laborers and farmers	1.3	5.3	4.0
Service workers	13.4	5.3	16.0
Household workers	2.8	—	—
Students	5.5	10.5	4.0
Housewives	2.8	5.3	12.0
Illegal occupations	5.0	5.3	16.0
Other (retired, etc.)	1.8	—	4.0
Total (percent)	100.0	100.0	100.0
Total (number)	(396)	(19)	(25)

Table 12.6 Race, by Social Class

SOCIAL CLASS	WHITE	BLACK	OTHER MINORITIES
Elite (royalty, etc.)	1.7%	—	3.5%
Upper (rich)	5.4	9.1%	—
Upper-middle	50.7	45.5	6.9
Lower-middle	33.2	36.4	55.2
Lower	2.7	4.5	17.2
Déclassé	6.3	4.5	17.2
Total (percent)	100.0	100.0	100.0
Total (number)	(410)	(22)	(29)

Table 12.7 Major Ethnic Character Roles and Occupations, by Program Types

CHARACTER	ETHNICITY	OCCUPATION/ROLE	DRAMATIC ROLE*
Cartoon comedy (Hong Kong Phooey, Daffy Duck, Plasticman and Baby Plas, Heckle and Jeckle, Bugs Bunny, Popeye, Flintstone Comedy Show, The Fonz, The Heathcliff and Dingbat Show, Underdog, Tom and Jerry).			
Prof. Presto	Black	Magician	V
Valerie	Black	Musician	OM
Fat Albert	Black	Male child	OM
Dum Donald	Black	Male child	OM
Spike	Irish	Dog	OM
Hidia Frankenstone	Slavic	Housewife	OM
Sea Dog Pirate	English	Dog	OM
Vampire	Germanic	Vampire	V
Jeckle	English	Treasure hunter	OM
Commander McBragg	English	Spy	H
Baron Lafeet LaCheat	French	Car racer	V
Blacque Jacque Shellacque	French	Thief	V
Captain Dunk	English	Ghost/pirate	V
Matador	Mexican	Matador	OM
Speedy Gonzales	Mexican	Mouse	OM
Olive Oyl	Spanish	Dancer	OM
Little Mouse	Mexican	Mouse	OM
Fruit Man	Puerto Rican	Clock thief	V
Mummy	Egyptian	Mummy	OM
Hula-Hula	Hawaiian	Friend/assistant	OM
Captain Caveman	Other	Comic superhero	H
Rocky James	Other	Crook	V
Shadow	Other	Spy	V
Crime/action/adventure drama (Superstretch and Microwoman, Godzilla, Batman, Superfriends, New Adventures of Mighty Mouse, Tarzan/Lone Ranger Hour, Force Five, Spiderwoman, Starblazers, Thunderbirds, Johnny Quest).			
Brock	Black	Ship's crew	OM
Superstretch	Black	Superhero	H
Microwoman	Black	Superhero	H
Scott	Black	Superhero	H
Brown Hornet	Black	Comic superhero	H
Dr. Copernicus	English	Scientist	OM
Mike Kelly	Irish	Settler	OM
Red Dog	English	Ship's crew	OM
Mr. Henry	English	Ship's crew	OM
Captain Kid	English	Captain/pirate	OM
Oil Can Harry	Arab	High priest	V
Set	Arab	God of Evil	OM
Pearl Pure Haititi	Arab/Egyptian	Queen	OM
Samurai	Japanese	Superhero	H
Hadji	Asian	Friend/assistant	OM

Table 12.7   Major Ethnic Character Roles and Occupations, by Program Types (cont.)

CHARACTER	ETHNICITY	OCCUPATION/ROLE	DRAMATIC ROLE*
Chief	Spanish-speaking	Kidnapper/treasure hunter	V
Spy	Russian	Spy	V
Dr. Frankenstein	Germanic	Doctor/scientist	OM
Shara	Other (Incan)	Amazon leader	V
Tonto	Native American	Assistant/sidekick	OM
Deslock	Other (Gamelon)	Leader, other race	V
Princess Areo	Other (uncertain)	Assistant to hero	OM
Tana	Other (caveperson)	Daughter	OM
Dr. Ores	Other (blue-skinned)	Evildoer	V

Other dramatic programs (Carrascolendas, Qué Pasa, USA?, Villa Allegre).

Cobby	Black	Male child	H
Warner	Black	Male child	OM
Gary	Jewish	Husband	OM
Juana	Cuban	Mother/housewife	OM
Abuela	Cuban	Grandmother	OM
Patria	Cuban	Cousin	OM
Morris	Mexican	Male child	H
Don Rafael	Mexican	Barber	OM
Señor Capitan	Mexican	Ship's captain	OM
Campamocha	Mexican	Runs fix-it shop	OM
Luis	Mexican	Male child	OM

Other informational (Snipets, Cap't. Kangaroo, For Kids Only, Time Out, Ask NBC News, Drawing Power, Get Off Your Block, Jabberwocky, Big Blue Marble, Villa Allegre).

Roy	Black	Cast member	NA
Boys (3 times)	Black	Male child	NA
Bill Cosby	Black	Host	NA
Allieu Massaquoi	Black	Youth counsellor	NA
Doug Pendarvis	Black	Director, training center	NA
Gary Coleman	Black	Actor/narrator	NA
Tiffany	Black	Student	NA
Kari Page	Black	Animator	NA
Sara Clutchfield	Black	Host/interviewer	NA
Carl	Black	Talk-show host	NA
Tony Hayes	English	Seaman on the Q.E. II	NA
Boy teen	Chinese	Busboy	NA
J.P. Wang	Chinese	Host	NA
Sue Lin	Chinese	Female child	NA
Gloria	Mexican	Female child	NA
Carlos	Mexican	Male child	NA

*Dramatic roles: H = hero; V = villain; OM = other major character; and NA = not applicable—non dramatic role.

Thus we see a perpetuation of stereotypical thinking about minorities and foreigners—especially in cartoon comedies and other animated dramatic forms. Even the names chosen perpetuate these same stereotypes—the English lord and lady, the Hawaiian Hula-Hula, the Japanese Samurai, the French baron, and the German Dr. Frankenstein. Since nearly three-fourths of all segments studied were in animated form, these stereotypical portrayals become a significant factor in all commerical children's television.

This is not true of programs originally produced for Public Broadcasting—"Carrascolendas," "¿Qué Pasa, USA?," and "Villa Allegre"—whose dramatic segments deal more with real people and real situations.

13 MINORITY VALUE ORIENTATIONS: GOALS AND MEANS TO GOALS

The goals to which various characters aspire, whether positive, socially accepted ones (love, honesty and justice) or socially disapproved of (power, hatred and revenge), provide an index to the kinds of value orientations communicated by commercial children's TV. In this analysis, only major dramatic characters could be classified according to their goals in the stories. There were 490 such major characters classified as either heroes, villains, or other major characters. Of these, only 58 (11.8 percent) were identified by ethnicity, precluding detailed statistical comparisons of ethnic groups by specific goal orientations.

Table 13.1 shows the overall emphasis on various goal aspirations for all major dramatic characters. These have been grouped into categories of self-goals and altruistic goals, with the latter representing slightly more than one-half of goals sought.

The two major altruistic goals of justice (duty and the preservation of law and order), and love (friendship, companionship, and affection) account for 30 percent of all character goals. The following examples illustrate how these are evidenced in the stories studied.

Justice/duty: Batman stopping brain creatures from destroying the earth; Thundarr stopping man apes from destroying the city; Plasticman stopping plant monsters; and the police officer wants to stop all crime in his precinct.

Love/affection/friendship: Barbapapa shears sheep to keep them cool; the pet dog runs to warn its master about crooks; Gorilla mothers Baby Plas; Cupid shoots animals with arrows; and Dixie Mouse wants to give Mighty Mite a home.

Self-indulgences, the accumulation of wealth, and hatred or revenge goals led the list of self-goals, accounting for about 27 percent of all goals. Examples of these follow.

Table 13.1 Goals of All Major Dramatic Characters

GOALS	NUMBER	PERCENT
Self		
Self-indulgence (satisfaction of impulses, leisure, escape)	54	11.0
Self-preservation (safety)	42	8.6
Wealth (material success)	40	8.2
Hatred (revenge, destruction, spite)	38	7.7
Fame (reputation, prestige, popularity)	16	3.3
Power (mastery over others)	15	3.1
Thrill (adventure, pleasure)	14	2.8
Other	4	0.8
Total, self-goals	223	45.5
Altruistic		
Justice (duty, preservation of law and order)	81	16.5
Love (friendship, companionship, affection)	67	13.7
Work (industriousness)	18	3.7
Home (marriage, family, parental duties)	16	3.3
Patriotism (devotion to country)	14	2.9
Knowledge (education, enlightenment)	11	2.3
Devotion to a cause or group	10	2.0
Other (respect for others, aesthetic values, idealism, brotherhood, freedom, morality, religion)	26	5.2
Total, altruistic goals	243	49.6
Unclassifiable, uncertain	24	4.9
Total, all goals	490	100.0

Self-indulgences: Daffy doesn't want to fly south for winter; Olive wants to make Popeye jealous; the Jetsons want to enjoy a second honeymoon undisturbed; and Cat seeks to catch and eat the canary.

Wealth: Crook wants to steal Richie's money; Daffy wants to collect $1,000 in a contest; owner of a whale wants 50 percent of the profits from a whale album; and the robber baron tries to hold a princess for ransom.

Hatred/revenge: Strongman wants to get Shaggy and Scooby for hitting him with a ball; the leader of man apes wants to destroy the humans' city; the plant monster wants to eat all plants in the city; Coyote wants to destroy Road Runner; and Bluto hates Popeye and fights him.

Self-preservation was another important goal of the characters, accounting for 9 percent of all the goals classified. This results from the many stories of interpersonal rivalry and the chase sequences in cartoon comedies, where the major goal seems only to be self-preservation.

More idealistic and complex goals such as a searching for aesthetic values, freedom, morality, and ethical and religious values were seldom sought. This is a reflection of the rather simplistic nature of most cartoons and other dramatic fare presented to children.

For all characters, negative value orientations are outnumbered by positive ones. Nevertheless, self-indulgence, wealth, hatred, fame, power, and thrill seeking account collectively for about one-third of the total of goals sought after by the characters.

Looking at racial and ethnic characterizations, there are few major differences in goal orientations. The primary differences occur between human characters and animal or other nonhuman characters—the latter are more involved in self-goals and less in altruistic ones (see Table 13.2).

The table affirms the findings with respect to the distribution of hero-villain roles. Blacks show the highest proportion of altruistic goal seeking (six of nine characters); whites show about six out of ten and other minorities about the same. These differences are not statistically significant ones, however, as the total number of minority characters is small, and generalizations become difficult to make. Ethnically, Arabs, Europeans, and other ethnic characters are portrayed as least concerned with altruistic goals (eight of 26 in these groups seek altruistic goals).

Table 13.2 Race and Ethnicity, by Goals Sought

CLASSIFICATION	SELF-GOALS (NUMBER)	ALTRUISTIC GOALS (NUMBER)	PERCENT ALTRUISTIC*
Race			
White	90	141	61
Black	3	6	67
Other minorities	7	11	61
Uncertain	3	2	40
Animals	94	56	37
Other nonhuman	26	27	51
Ethnic Group			
Blacks	3	7	70
Europeans	13	6	32
Arabs	3	1	25
Asians	1	2	67
Hispanics	6	9	60
Other ethnics	2	1	33
Not identified ethnically	195	217	53
All characters	223	243	52

*Percent of all in each group that used altruistic goals; caution should be exercised in interpretations because of the small numbers on which these percentages are based.

GOAL-SEEKING BEHAVIORS

Of the 490 major dramatic characters, 445 were classified both as to major goals in the stories and the means used in attempting to achieve their goals.

Looking at all characters, the two major behavioral means of achieving goals were violence (30 percent of means) and personal industry or intelligent planning (26 percent). These were followed by trickery or deceit (11 percent) and dependence on others (10 percent). The use of duly established authority, persuasion, and personal charm, or simply attaining goals through luck or fate, each accounted for 5 percent or less of means used by characters seeking goals (see Table 13.3).

Ethnically identified characters did not differ significantly from nonethnic characters in goal seeking, although they did show a slightly greater tendency to use personal charm and personal industry, and a slightly lesser tendency to use violence, authority, luck, trickery, and dependence on others (see Table 13.4).

As for means used to achieve different types of goals (see Table 13.5), ethnic characters utilized violence and personal industry to a greater extent than others in striving for self-goals. For altruistic goals, ethnic characters tended more toward personal industry and personal charm than did nonethnics—the latter more frequently utilizing violence. For both ethnic and nonethnic characters, violence and trickery were most frequently used in attempts to achieve self-goals, whereas personal industry and intelligent planning were more frequently used for altruistic goals.

THE ATTAINMENT OF GOALS

Another possible indicator of value orientation is the extent to which ethnic and nonethnic groups achieve goals. Of all characters classified for goal seeking, 62 percent were seen as achieving their goals. By type of character, larger proportions of both blacks and other minorities achieved their goals than did whites. Least likely to achieve goals were other nonhuman characters (see Table 13.6). Other ethnics (especially Europeans and Arabs—who were more villainous as a group) were shown less often as achieving desired goals. This reflects the distribution of heroes and villains (noted earlier) showing larger proportions of black heroes, and greater proportions of other ethnics and nonhuman characters as villains.

For those who did not achieve desired goals, the barriers to achievement were also looked at (see Table 13.7). The major barriers for all characters' goal attainment was violence from others—whether or not

Table 13.3 Means Used in Goal Seeking, by Type of Character

MEANS USED	WHITES	ALL MINORITIES	ANIMALS	OTHER NONHUMANS	ALL CHARACTERS
Violence	27.5%	21.9%	33.1%	36.7%	29.9%
Authority (law, police)	7.2	6.3	—	12.2	5.4
Luck/fate/chance	4.9	6.2	5.6	6.1	5.4
Trickery/deceit	7.7	3.1	19.0	6.1	10.8
Personal charm	4.1	9.4	1.4	2.1	3.4
Persuasion	3.1	3.1	6.3	—	3.8
Dependence on others	9.9	12.5	9.2	10.2	9.9
Personal industry/intelligence	29.3	25.0	21.9	22.5	25.8
Other	6.3	12.5	3.5	4.1	5.6
Total (percent)	100.0	100.0	100.0	100.0	100.0
Total (number)	(222)	(32)	(142)	(49)	(445)

103

effective. Although for one-fourth of goal-seeking efforts, no discernible barriers were noted, 37 percent of ethnic and 40 percent of nonethnic characters were opposed by violence. No other major important barriers were noted for either group.

Table 13.4 Means Used in Goal Seeking, by Ethnic and Nonethnic Characters

MEANS USED	ETHNIC CHARACTERS	NONETHNIC CHARACTERS
Violence	28.6%	29.9%
Authority	4.1	5.8
Luck/fate/chance	4.1	5.5
Trickery/deceit	8.2	11.5
Personal charm	10.2	2.4
Persuasion	4.1	3.7
Dependence on others	6.1	9.7
Personal industry/intelligence	28.6	26.0
Other	6.0	5.5
Total (percent)	100.0	100.0
Total (number)	(49)	(381)

Table 13.5 Means Used by Ethnic and Non-Ethnic Groups to Achieve Self and Altruistic Goals

MEANS USED	SELF-GOALS		ALTRUISTIC GOALS	
	ETHNIC CHARACTERS	NONETHNIC CHARACTERS	ETHNIC CHARACTERS	NONETHNIC CHARACTERS
Violence	50.0%	41.0%	4.4%	19.7%
Authority	3.8	1.6	4.3	9.6
Luck/fate/chance	—	4.9	8.7	6.1
Trickery/deceit	11.6	19.7	4.3	4.0
Personal charm	3.8	1.1	17.4	3.5
Persuasion	—	4.4	8.7	3.0
Dependence on others	7.7	12.6	4.3	7.1
Personal industry/intelligence	15.4	12.0	43.5	38.9
Other	7.7	2.7	4.4	8.1
Total (percent)	100.0	100.0	100.0	100.0
Total (number)	(26)	(183)	(23)	(198)

Table 13.6 Attainment of Goals, by Race and Ethnicity

| CLASSIFICATION | WAS GOAL ATTAINED? | | TOTAL CLASSIFIED |
	NUMBER "YES"	PERCENT "YES"	
Race			
White	143	61.9	231
Black	7	77.8	9
Other minorities	12	66.7	18
Other humans, race unknown	4	80.0	5
Animal characters	92	61.3	150
Other nonhumans	30	56.6	53
Ethnic Group			
Blacks	7	70.0	10
Europeans	9	47.4	19
Arabs	1	25.0	4
Asians	3	100.0	3
Hispanics	12	80.0	15
Other ethnics	1	33.3	3
Not identified ethnically	255	61.9	412
All characters	288	61.8	466

Table 13.7 Barriers to Achieving Goals, by Ethnic and Nonethnic Characters

BARRIER	ETHNIC CHARACTERS	CHARACTERS NOT IDENTIFIED ETHNICALLY	ALL CHARACTERS
None, undefinable	33.3%	23.6%	24.7%
Violence	37.0	40.5	40.1
Authority	5.6	2.4	2.8
Luck/fate/chance	1.9	7.5	6.9
Trickery/deceit by others	3.7	6.8	6.4
Being charmed by others	—	—	—
Being persuaded	1.9	0.5	0.6
Personal deficiencies (physical or mental)	3.7	5.6	5.4
Personal industry, intelligence of others	9.2	9.0	9.0
Other	3.7	4.1	4.1
Total (percent)	100.0	100.0	100.0
Total (number)	(54)	(412)	(466)

14 PERSONALITY TRAITS OF MINORITY AND MAJORITY CHARACTERS

The final measure utilized in the analysis of ethnic portrayals was one focusing on several selected personality traits (and on some physical characteristics) displayed by the characters. Table 14.1 summarizes the mean scores on 12 personality scales and on three scales of physical appearance, for all heroes and villains, and for ethnic heroes and villains.

Hero and villain characters differed significantly on almost all scales, whether they were ethnic or nonethnic characters. The largest differences, of course, appear in the evaluative measures that are highly correlated with the good-bad conceptions used to classify heroes and villains. The scale results confirm this classification. Thus, heroes were rated as more kind, unselfish, and honest, but also as stronger, and more intelligent, active, agile, peaceful and warm than villains. Physically, they were rated as thinner, more handsome, and better dressed than were villains.

Notably, ethnic heroes and villains seem to be depicted with more extreme characteristics than are all heroes and villains. That is, the scale-point differences between ethnic heroes and villains were greater—on ten of the 12 personality scales—than between nonethnic heroes and villains. Ethnic characters seem more likely to be cast as either superheroes or archvillains.

Primarily because of the small numbers of ethnic characters in the analysis, only a few significant differences were found between the mean scores of ethnic heroes and other heroes, of ethnic villains and other villains, and of all other major ethnic and nonethnic characters (see Table 14.2).

Some consistent tendencies were noted however, with ethnic heroes tending to be more serious and active than nonethnic heroes. Moreover, ethnic villains tended to be more cruel, dishonest, and selfish, and

Table 14.1 Personality Traits of the Characters: Comparing Ethnic and All Heroes and Villains

PERSONALITY SCALE	ALL HEROES	ALL VILLAINS	SIGNIFICANCE	ETHNIC HEROES	ETHNIC VILLAINS	SIGNIFICANCE
Serious-comic	3.0	3.1	—	2.8	2.9	—
Strong-weak	2.1	2.5	(a)	2.0	2.3	—
Unselfish-selfish	2.3	4.1	(a)	2.4	4.4	(a)
Good-bad	1.9	4.3	(a)	1.9	4.5	(a)
Peaceful-violent	3.3	4.2	(a)	2.9	4.2	(a)
Kind-cruel	2.6	4.1	(a)	2.4	4.5	(a)
Intelligent-stupid	2.3	2.9	(a)	2.0	2.9	(b)
Independent-dependent	2.8	2.1	(c)	2.1	2.1	—
Warm-cool	2.5	3.6	(a)	2.6	3.7	(b)
Honest-dishonest	2.9	3.8	(a)	2.9	4.3	(a)
Active-passive	1.5	2.0	(a)	1.2	2.4	(a)
Agile-clumsy	2.3	2.9	(a)	1.9	3.0	(a)
Thin-fat	2.7	3.2	(a)	2.9	3.3	(d)
Handsome-ugly	2.7	3.5	(a)	2.8	3.5	(b)
Well dressed-sloppy	2.5	2.8	(a)	2.2	2.6	—
Number in group	(111)	(95)		(8)	(13)	

Note: In this table and Tables 14.2 and 14.3, figures are mean scores of five-point scales, with 1 corresponding to the left-hand adjective and 5 to the right-hand one. For example, here, on the third scale: all 111 heroes averaged more unselfish (2.3) than all 95 villains, who were rated as quite selfish (4.1). Similarly, 13 ethnic villains rated as even more selfish (4.4), compared with ethnic heroes (2.4). Differences between groups were tested by using the Mann-Whitney "U" test and are reported in the table as follows: (a) P < .01; (b) p < .05; (c) p < .10; (d) p < .20.

Table 14.2 Personality Traits of the Characters: Comparing Ethnic and Nonethnic Heroes, Villains, and Others

PERSONALITY SCALE	ETHNIC HEROES	OTHER HEROES	ETHNIC VILLAINS	OTHER VILLAINS	ETHNIC OTHERS	NONETHNIC OTHERS
Serious-comic	2.8	3.1 (d)	2.9	3.1	3.0	3.4 (b)
Strong-weak	2.0	2.1	2.3	2.6 (c)	2.6	2.8 (c)
Unselfish-selfish	2.4	2.3	4.4	4.0 (c)	3.1	2.9
Good-bad	1.9	1.9	4.5	4.2	2.5	2.6
Peaceful-violent	2.9	3.4	4.2	4.2	2.7	3.0 (d)
Kind-cruel	2.4	2.6	4.5	4.1 (b)	2.8	3.0 (c)
Intelligent-stupid	2.0	2.3	2.8	2.9	2.6	2.9 (d)
Independent-dependent	2.1	2.3	2.1	2.1	2.8	2.8
Warm-cool	2.6	2.5	3.7	3.5	2.5	2.5
Honest-dishonest	2.9	2.9	4.3	3.7 (b)	3.0	3.1 (d)
Active-passive	1.2	1.6 (d)	2.4	1.9 (b)	2.3	2.1
Agile-clumsy	1.9	2.3	3.0	2.9	2.8	2.7
Thin-fat	2.9	2.7	3.3	3.2	2.8	2.9
Handsome-ugly	2.8	2.7	3.5	3.5	2.8	3.0 (d)
Well dressed-sloppy	2.2	2.5	2.6	2.8	2.5	2.7 (b)
Number in group	(8)	(103)	(13)	(82)	(37)	(247)

stronger, but less active than were their nonethnic counterparts. Other ethnic characters tended to be more serious than other nonethnic characters. They also tended to be stronger and more selfish, peaceful, kind, and intelligent than their nonethnic counterparts.

Comparing each specific ethnic group to all nonethnic characters (see Table 14.3), blacks were rated slightly more serious, peaceful, kind, and intelligent than all nonethnics, whereas Europeans were rated as more selfish, cruel, cool, dishonest, and passive. Physically, the latter were somewhat less agile and less handsome than all nonethnics. Hispanics were shown as somewhat stronger, and more peaceful, kind, and warm. No differences between all other ethnics (i.e., a group combining Asians, Arabs, and others) and nonethnics approached statistical significance.

It would appear, then, from the foregoing analysis that personality traits are assigned primarily to various dramatic roles and secondarily to ethnic groups. However, although the numbers are small, the tendency seems to be to show ethnic heroes as more heroic than nonethnic heroes and ethnic villains as more villainous than their nonethnic counterparts.

Table 14.3 Personality Traits of the Characters: Comparing Specific Ethnic Groups to All Nonethnic Characters

PERSONALITY SCALE	BLACKS		EUROPEANS		HISPANICS		ALL OTHERS		NONETHNICS
Serious-comic	2.8	(c)	2.9	(b)	3.0	(d)	3.1		3.3
Strong-weak	2.3		2.6		2.4		2.6		2.6
Unselfish-selfish	2.9		3.8	(a)	2.9		3.3		3.0
Good-bad	2.2	(c)	3.3	(b)	2.5		3.2		2.8
Peaceful-violent	2.6	(c)	3.4		2.6	(b)	3.5		3.3
Kind-cruel	2.7		3.5	(b)	2.6	(b)	3.3		3.1
Intelligent-stupid	2.3	(c)	2.7		2.8		2.6		2.8
Independent-dependent	2.7		2.3		2.6		2.8		2.5
Warm-cool	2.7		3.0	(c)	2.3	(b)	3.1	(d)	2.7
Honest-dishonest	3.0		3.6	(b)	3.1		3.1		3.2
Active-passive	1.8		2.4	(b)	2.2		2.0		1.9
Agile-clumsy	2.3	(d)	2.9		2.8		2.6		2.7
Thin-fat	2.8		3.0		2.9		2.9		2.9
Handsome-ugly	2.7		3.3	(c)	2.8		2.7		3.0
Well dressed-sloppy	2.5		2.5		2.5	(d)	2.4	(c)	2.7
Number in group	(11)		(21)		(16)		(10)		(432)

Note: The comparison is made of each ethnic group to nonethnic characters. Thus, on the scale unselfish-selfish, no significant differences were found between blacks and nonethnics, Hispanics and nonethnics, or others and nonethnics; whereas, Europeans were rated as significantly more selfish (3.8) than nonethnic characters (3.0), with a probability of < .01.

15 SUMMARY: PORTRAYALS OF MINORITIES

Perhaps the most significant finding of this study of the portrayal of racial and ethnic minorities on commercial children's television lies in the small numbers of minority characters. This lack of recognition of all ethnic minorities is clearly evident in the summary data below:

- 184 ethnic characters represent 16.1 percent of 1,145 characters
- 42 black ethnics represent 3.7 percent of 1,145 characters
- 41 black humans represent 5.4 percent of 758 human characters
- 35 Hispanics represent 3.1 percent of 1,145 characters
- 9 Asians represent 0.8 percent of 1,145 characters
- 77 Europeans represent 6.7 percent of 1,145 characters

Ethnic minorities also are less often found in major roles:

- 58 ethnic characters represent 11.8 percent of 490 major dramatic characters
- 10 black characters represent 2.0 percent of 490 major dramatic characters
- 18 nonblack minorities represent 3.7 percent of 490 major dramatic characters

In hero and villain roles, black ethnics are more often cast as heroes than as villains, but their proportions in both roles are low. Other ethnics are more often cast as villains:

- 5 black heroes represent 4.5 percent of 111 heroes
- 1 black villain represents 1.1 percent of 95 villains
- 3 other ethnics represent 2.7 percent of 111 heroes
- 12 other ethnics represent 12.6 percent of 95 villains

Black and other minorities are also less frequently portrayed as employed than are white characters:

- 344 out of 659 white characters (52.2 percent) were shown as employed
- 15 out of 41 black characters (36.6 percent) were shown as employed
- 16 out of 47 other minorites (34.0 percent) were shown as employed

When shown as employed, both black and white characters are most often shown in professional and managerial jobs, whereas other minorities are more likely to be portrayed as craftsmen, laborers, or service workers.

In value orientations, black ethnics seem more likely to pursue altruistic goals than do other ethnic groups (reflecting the tendency for blacks to be cast as heroes rather than villains). Minority characters, in general, are less likely to use violence to accomplish goals, but are more apt to depend on others, use personal charm, or accomplish goals through luck or circumstance.

Few major differences were found between ethnic and nonethnic heroes in terms of their personality traits. However, ethnic villains were seen as somewhat stronger, and more selfish, cruel, and dishonest than nonethnic villains.

Also, although the differences were not large, black ethnics tended to be portrayed as somewhat more serious, peaceful, and intelligent than nonethnics. European ethnics, on the other hand, were seen as more selfish, cruel, and dishonest, as well as more serious, cool, passive, and ugly than nonethnics. Hispanics characters were rated as more peaceful, kind, and warm than nonethnic characters.

Although blacks have reached some level of respect when portrayed (i.e., as hero characters, in occupational roles, value orientations, and personality traits), they are so outnumbered overall by others in these roles that their absence offsets this respect afforded them. The same hold true for Hispanics. As for other ethnic groups, they have achieved neither adequate recognition nor treatment that one might expect all minorities would be accorded.

Except for those programs which have been specifically designed to provide information and more realistic portrayals of minorities ("Carrascolendas," "¿Qué Pasa, USA?," "Villa Allegre," and "The Fat Albert Show"), or the newer genre of short information "drop-in" programs (e.g., "Ask NBC News," "Time Out," and "Snipets"), commercial children's televison tends more to avoid racial or ethnic messages than to deal with them adequately or realistically. Race and nationality themes, for example, represented only 3 percent of 352 major and minor subject classifications.

Cartoon-comedy programs contain the most blatant ethnic stereo-types. These programs also avoid the portrayal of black characters, and frequently provide cruel stereotypes of other ethnic minorities. And cartoon comedies alone amount to nearly one-half of all program time in children's TV. In addition, almost two-thirds of all characters appear either in cartoon comedies or animated-action or adventure dramas.

In terms of both the recognition and treatment of racial and ethnic minorities, it is fair to say that those programs originally produced for the Public Broadcasting Service (some of which are now being carried by commercial stations) have led the way in providing more reasonable and balanced images of black and other ethnic groups. But even including these programs, commercial children's TV does not approach the level of recognition of these groups that has been reported in programming for adults according to prior research over the past decade.

Commercial children's television can only be seen as a major barrier in the battle for recognition of and respect for ethnic groups in this country.

IV
Family and
Kinship Portrayals

16 THE FAMILY AND TELEVISION PORTRAYALS

The purpose of this chapter is to summarize briefly some of the relevant sociological literature related to the family and to look at the few studies that have been done on the portrayals of family life on television. In general, very little research on television portrayals of the family has been conducted.

Television itself has been described as a member of the family (Singer and Singer, 1977). But no member of the family, except perhaps the mother, commands the attention of the child for such long periods of time during the day. Television programming, therefore, needs examination for the lessons it is teaching to the child as an integral part of the family unit.

APPROACHES TO THE STUDY OF THE FAMILY

When studying the family on television, several theoretical approaches might be used as models for the analysis. In the past several decades, at least five approaches have been developed that help in our analysis. These have been summarized by Allen (1978) as follows:

1. The "institutional" approach considers the origin and evolution of families, through cross-cultural and cross-historical comparisons.
2. The "structural-functional" approach views the family as a social system and focuses on both its internal system relationships and external relationships with other societal subsystems.
3. The "interactional" approach attempts to interpret family phenomena in terms of internal, interpersonal processes.
4. The "situational" approach views the family as a social situation which influences member behaviors.

5. The "developmental" approach views the family and its members as moving through a life cycle or series of developmental stages.

Of these five approaches, perhaps the most attention has been given to three—the interactional, the structural-functional, and the developmental.

In this study, the analyses of roles, interaction, and dominance patterns in conflict and nonconflict situations illustrate the symbolic-interaction approach. The structure and functions of the family unit are studied in the analysis of kinship relations, child-rearing functions, the way families work together in goal attainment, and the way they behave in conflict situations. The developmental approach is considered by examining the stages of family development portrayed in the programs. Eight stages are described by Duvall (1971, reviewed in Eshelman [1974, p.73]): stage 1: married couples (without children); stage 2: childbearing families (oldest child is up to 30 months); stage 3: families with preschool children (oldest child is two-and-one-half–six years); stage 4: families with school children (oldest child is 6–13 years); stage 5: families with teenagers (oldest child is 13–20 years); stage 6: families as launching centers (from first child's being gone to last child's leaving home); stage 7: middle-aged parents (from an empty nest to retirement); stage 8: aging family members (from retirement to death of both spouses).

THE CHANGING FAMILY STRUCTURE IN THE UNITED STATES

When studying television images, it is easier to make a comparison with the real world in some areas than in others. Thus, by using relatively up-to-date and accurate census statistics, it is not difficult to discover whether television presents an accurate picture of the current occupational statuses of men and women. Although some such statistics are also available for family compositions, the shifting patterns of family life are not so easily defined.

This situation is illustrated in some of the figures discussed below. They are presented to provide some guidelines to this real world to which we may refer in the analysis of the family and kinship relations depicted on children's television.

Traditionally, the American family has developed as a monogamous, independent family unit in which the average age for marriage of males is 22 and for females 20. In the last two decades, there has been a trend toward earlier marriage. Also, the traditions of inheritance and authority have given the most importance to male family members. Many sociologists, however, have noted an increasing trend toward instability in the family system.

A report cited by Stencel (1979) in *The Changing American Family* produced some statistics concerning current family patterns in the United States:

> Three groups—childless couples, couples whose children are grown, and households headed by women—now represent nearly a quarter of all family groups; another quarter falls into such categories as communes, affiliated monogamous families sharing a common household, unmarried couples, single persons alone, single persons living together for economic or convenience reasons without forming a true "family," and stable homosexual couples. Finally, 4 percent of the families still are reported to be "extended," those in which grandparents or such other relatives as uncles or aunts are part of the household. This means that fewer than half of all American families fall into the category of a traditional nuclear family—father, mother and children living together in their own household.

By family type, estimates indicate that approximately 45 percent of family-kinship units consist of intact nuclear families. The table below has been abstracted from figures presented by Reiss (1979). The data are for family distributions in the United States in 1976.

Type	Percent
Nuclear family intact	45
Nuclear family "remarried"	10
Nuclear dyad (husband-wife alone)	15
Single-parent family	15
Kin networks (extended family)	2
All other (single, widowed, divorced, communal, or unmarried parents)	13
	100

These figures give us some rough guidelines for a comparison of family types on children's television. However, a recent *Boston Globe* article (October 28, 1981, p. 53) reported that there is even less emphasis on the nuclear family today:

> Things are different now. According to the U.S. Census Bureau, the "typical" two-parent family represents fewer than one-third of U.S. households. Nearly 30 percent of the population consists of married couples with no children. More than 8 percent of all families with children are headed by a single adult—and the majority are headed by women. More than 25 percent of American households—one in four—consist of one person living alone or with non-family members. The number of unmarried couples living together has tripled in 10 years.
>
> Widowhood and the spiralling divorce rate has created countless one-person and single-parent households. Couples are choosing to have fewer children—or no children at all.

Traditional and Emerging Family Structures

Petrich and Chadderdon (1969) point out that the structure of the American family is in a state of flux, but that authorities disagree regarding the inevitability of trends away from traditional patterns. They provide (p. 375) an ideal-type construct, with the polar points being represented as the traditional family and the emerging family:

The Traditional Family	The Emerging Family
1. Sees compliance with duty as a goal.	1. Sees personal happiness as a goal.
2. Follows tradition.	2. Desires innovation.
3. Definitely differentiates between male and female roles, and between adult and child roles.	3. Accepts an interchange of female and male roles.
4. Has a definitely established hierarchy of communication channels and exhibits controlled affectional communication.	4. Has open communication channels with frequent affectional communication.
5. Considers kinship the basic social bond.	5. Develops social bonds with many groups.
6. Achieves status as total family regardless of individual skills and accomplishments.	6. Allows different status levels for individuals within the family.
7. Participates in outside groups on a family basis.	7. Participates in a wide variety of groups on an individual basis.
8. Places emphasis on objectives established by the authority figure or by tradition.	8. Places emphasis on individual objectives.
9. Is a major influence in economic, educational, recreational, and religious functions.	9. Is willing to relinquish its influence in economic, educational, recreational, and religious functions to other groups.
10. Bases behavior, discipline, and obedience patterns on authority and customs.	10. Bases behavior, discipline and obedience patterns on bonds of affection.
11. Is authoritarian and based on the subordination of the individual members to the authority figure.	11. Is developmental and based on the worth and developmental stage of individuals.

Benson (1971) believes that the typical American family is conventionally identified with suburban life, since many families were moving away from cities toward the beginning of the 1970s. He notes (p. 3) that as people were scrambling to the suburbs, marriage problems and parent-child relationships were affected by the changes, but these consequences have not drastically altered the fundamental basis for family life:

> Traditional family customs and the problems associated with them have remained remarkably stable. They do change, of course, but slowly—except at critical times in history. It is possible that we are now living in such a critical period, but we cannot be too sure about that. The fall of the traditional family has been predicted repeatedly in the past, and it has repeatedly survived. Apparently it meets human needs as well as any alternative yet devised, but obviously it does not satisfy them so well that the search for something better is dropped altogether. The search never seems to end.

FAMILY PORTRAYALS ON TV

Relatively few research studies have been conducted to examine family portrayals on television. The most recent content analysis that focused on the family was published by Greenberg (1980) in his book *Life on Television: Content Analyses of U.S. TV Drama.* Greenberg et al. looked at "Family Role Structures and Interactions on Commercial Television." In addition, Greenberg and his associates conducted two other studies, which were titled "Three Seasons of Television Family Role Interactions," and "Black Family Interactions on Television."

In "Family Role Structures and Interactions on Commercial Television," the research focused on family structures and interaction patterns. Three basic modes of family interactions were developed from the theoretical literature: those going toward, going against, and going away from each other. Findings indicated that the patterns of family interaction shown on television were predominantly cooperative, with nearly 90 percent of all interactions coded as "going toward" (Greenberg et al., 1980, p. 156).

This study also found that 53 of 96 programs studied (55.2 percent) were related to the family in some way. Seventy-three family units were distributed as follows:

Unit	Number	Percent
Nuclear families	28	38.4
Single-parent families	19	26.0
Married couples	17	23.3
Others	9	12.3
	73	100.0

In addition, Greenberg's research (Greenberg et. al., 1980, pp. 158–159) concluded:

1. There are few pre-adolescent or early adolescent characters in television families.
2. Teenaged characters exhibit "independent-seeking" behaviors a great deal of the time, e.g., joking round and opposing their parents.
3. The portrayals of married couples support the following stereotypes: the husband directs the wife; the wife seeks support from the husband.

From this research Greenberg et al. surmised that because children are largely absent from television families, this might cause a child to question his or her own role in a real family. In addition, television portrayals of husbands, wives, and parents may be reinforcing stereotypical beliefs of children. In general, Greenberg et al. concluded that televised families reflect interactions that are common stereotypes. This study did not compare the observed family interactions with any data from the real world. Instead, the study described the televised family interactions to identify some aspects of social learning that may stem from the presentations.

As a basis for their "Three Seasons of Television Family Role Interactions," Greenberg et al. postulated that social learning about the family would be influenced to a greater extent when viewers followed the experiences of television characters over a period of time.

The study provided a "systematic identification of the predominant portrayals of family members and their interactions" in prime-time shows and syndicated afternoon series that featured families. The research included these conclusions (Greenberg et. al., 1980, p. 171):

1. The vast majority of fictional television characters do not have relatives appearing in the stories with them.
2. No particular configuration of family structure dominates; most common are families headed by a single parent or two parents, plus children; childless couples are nearly as frequent.
3. Divorce has increased each season; it has become equivalent to widowhood as a factor to account for single-parent families; first marriages account for half the adults, and one-fourth have never married.
4. Relatives outside the nuclear family are rare; nuclear family members account for 80 percent of all roleholders.
5. Males and females are equal in number in TV families.
6. Females and males are equal in initiating and receiving family role interactions.
7. Husbands and wives are the most active interacting TV family role pair.

8. Parents are more likely to interact with same-sex children, e.g., more father-son than father-daughter interactions.
9. Affiliative acts occur in TV families about eight times more often than conflictual acts.
10. Conflict is more heavily concentrated in husband-wife pairs and dyads that include a brother.
11. Offering information to others is the dominant mode of family interactions.
12. Parents are most likely to give directions; children least so.

The study assessed family roles and structures, but did not attempt to evaluate the quality or significance of the content.

In the conclusions of their study, Greenberg et al. noted that there is a special linkage between family roles and minority characterizations on TV: During the time period studied, nearly half of all regularly-appearing black TV characters were located on six situation comedies that featured family units. Greenberg and Neuendorf (1980) subsequently analyzed black-family interactions on television in a week of television during three consecutive seasons. They discovered that a black family appeared regularly on four or five shows. They also found (p. 181):

1. Typically, the black family would have a single parent.
2. Black family members were shown almost entirely in nuclear roles as fathers, sisters, wives, and children.
3. There were more black mothers than fathers.
4. The black son played a more major role than other children.
5. Conflict as the content of family interactions most frequently involved black wives and siblings.

Several other research efforts have been carried out that were concerned with aspects of families on television programs. In 1977, an international seminar was sponsored by the Prix Jeunesse Foundation in Munich. The lectures by researchers and practitioners in commercial television covered an examination of the portrayal of the relations between children and parents on television programs and the effects of television on the family unit. According to a summary of group discussions held at the seminar, written by Erentraud Homberg (1977), participants seemed to share these areas of concern in programming: avoiding overidealization and overdramatization; not shattering conventional family structures but carefully altering them; showing reality with its conflicts; conveying self-confidence and security; conveying democracy and solidarity in the family.

George Gerbner, in his lecture "Television and the Family" (cited in Homberg [1977, p. 14]) offered some generalizations from the hundreds of television programs he has studied over the past ten years:

The family is often depicted on American television, however usually in an unrealistic fashion—"soap operas," situation comedies. Children's programmes almost entirely avoid the subject of home and family. The difficult problems which might arise if this subject were treated don't fit into the commercial TV framework.

Gerbner concluded that TV exhibits conventional attitudes, firmly established stereotypes, and narrow concepts (including those relating to the family). He believes that heavy television viewers will be more influenced by these social messages than will light viewers.

In 1976, Miller and Beck posed this research question: "How do TV parents compare to real parents?" They conducted a study to determine how adolescents perceive television parents as compared to their own parents. Respondents were asked to select an answer from three possible choices that would resolve six situations typical of those that parents might face. Students responded by indicating which choice they perceived their own parents would make, which choice they felt each TV parent would make in each situation, and what they felt a good and a bad parent would do.

Miller and Beck (1976, pp. 327–328) noted:

> . . . respondents perceived their own parents as most often doing what they felt the good parent would do.
>
> Most television parents fared well, as they were perceived as doing what the good parent would do and not what the bad parent would do.
>
> The implications of this are that as parents most of these television characters are acceptable behavior models, and that these adolescents are *not* overwhelmed by the larger-than-life television parents at the expense of their perception of their own parents.

Foster (1964) compared father images on television to an idealized concept of the father. Her study was based on these assumptions (p. 354):

(a) children must have a male model in order to develop an adequate conception of the father role;
(b) traditionally, a child's own father provides the model;
(c) now, television presents multiple images of fathers which may or may not be different from the role conceived as ideal; and
(d) if these multiple television father images differ markedly from the image the actual father is attempting to depict, conflict in the child's development of the father concept could occur.

Foster selected 28 real fathers to score their concepts of an ideal father and of the fathers in four TV shows. Foster (1964, pp. 354–355) discovered:

A large number of statistically significant differences were found between the television fathers and the ideal father.

According to these results, television does present multiple father images that not only resemble one another but differ from the ideal father described by a group of real fathers.

Foster concluded (p. 355) that the impact of the portrayals of family-situation series on real family life is difficult to predict:

The social anxiety caused by the unknown effect of television warrants not only additional content analyses of the way in which social roles are portrayed in family television series, but also exploratory studies into the amount of realism children perceive in them.

In 1971, Bauer conducted a descriptive study of selected children's books and television programs to examine their presentation of supplemental family-life education. She reviewed a selection of 70 books and six television series, searching for content related to the family; the male and female role; sex and reproduction; and emotional development.

As a result of this research, Bauer (1971, p. 2896-A) stated these conclusions:

1. Family—The selected books and television equally presented a significant amount of variety covering the major aspects of family for the male and female child.
2. Role—The selected books and television supported the traditional view of male and female role.
3. Sex and reproduction—Television, particularly through the use of animals, is useful for presenting information to the younger child.
4. Emotional development—The selected television programs presented many aspects of this subject, but tended to do it in less depth and with less development than the books.

Bauer pointed out that in order to utilize the appropriate medium to fit the needs of the individual child, it is essential to critically appraise the book or the television program to properly meet a particular curricular goal.

Fisher (1974) explored marital and familial roles on television programs that were broadcast by the three major networks and that portrayed contemporary American families. He was specifically interested in the televised behaviors of the characters that functioned in roles of husband-father and wife-mother. Fisher sought to determine the kinds of behaviors spouses displayed toward each other and toward their children.

Fisher (1974, p. 599-A) looked at members of the immediate family in each portrayal, and found that in the televised material:

1. Familial role behaviors were usually conflict free, emphasizing affectionate and altruistic concerns for one's spouse and children.
2. Violent or disruptive behaviors were not evident.
3. The televised behaviors displayed little marital concern for financial or similar problems.
4. Television spouses helped each other, did little housework, and had few problems with the children.

According to Fisher, the marital- and familial-role behaviors can serve as imitative models for the viewer. TV was seen as an important vehicle for teaching nonmarried viewers about marital obligations and role expectations, as well as in offering possible solutions to those viewers who may be having marital difficulties. Overall, Fisher felt that the televised family portrayals seemed to emphasize socially approved cultural expectations.

Family Content in Children's Programming

Research regarding the family in children's television programming is extremely limited. Various studies have focused on the roles, behaviors, and statuses of characters in the programs, but there is little research that has specifically dealt with family units, or the roles and interactions of family members.

A succession of content-analytic studies commissioned by Action for Children's Television provides a minimal amount of information that is related to the use of a family for the program format and for subject matter in the children's shows. In a 1975 study of weekend children's television, only 2 percent of the television programs monitored were classified as family dramas. When analyzed by subject matter, 10 percent of the children's programs dealt with domestic concerns (e.g., marriage, home, and family). In a similar examination of children's commercial television after school, 17 out of 350 programs were family comedies. Of all the programs monitored, less than 5 percent were classified as family comedies (Barcus, 1977).

Later, in 1978, commercial children's television on weekends and weekday afternoons was analyzed (Barcus, 1978). Programs were evaluated in terms of program format and subject matter, with results being quite similar to those in 1975. Information about the family on children's TV is available only in this type of data. Many researchers have investigated the nature of male and female portrayals; aspects of program content, such as violence; and the composition and intent of commercials on children's TV. However, data about the family in children's programming remain scarce.

TELEVISION'S EFFECTS ON THE FAMILY

Although few content studies of family portrayals on television have been conducted, many research efforts relative to the issues of TV and the family do exist. The effect of TV on family life is one topic that has generated considerable interest. Meyer (1973, p. 26) notes:

> Recent long-term studies by Bronfenbrenner* indicate that parental and family influence in the development and socialization of children is steadily decreasing, while the influences of peer groups and television are rapidly increasing. To neglect the importance of television in the socialization process of children would be, according to Bronfenbrenner, a serious mistake . . .

In a review of the literature concerning the effects of television on children and adolescents, Comstock (1975, p. 27) cited the work of previous researchers and provided these conclusions:

1. Television for young persons is an experience largely devoid of direct parental influence.
2. Parents typically do not attempt to control quantity or character of viewing, although there are certainly restrictions in some families.
3. Parents often express concern, and the fact that parental efforts to ban certain programs and to stipulate the viewing of others increases when children approach adolescence suggests unarticulated alarm over television's competition as a socializing agent.
4. The family can hardly be said to be irrelevant because viewing and various attitudes and classes of behavior relevant to television have been found to be correlated with various family attributes other than race and income.

Many other researchers have offered insight into the nature of television and family life (McDonagh, 1950; Klineberg and Klapper, 1960; Blood, 1961; Barcus, 1969; Lewis and McMillen, 1972; McLeod, Atkin, and Chaffee, 1972; Brody et al., 1980).

Several studies have examined the family-related roles and behaviors of the characters on television and provided information that is related to the family and television. Many of the conclusions relate to male

---

*Here, the author cites Urie Bronfenbrenner, *Two Worlds of Childhood* (New York: Russell Sage, 1970).

and female roles in the family. For example, Long and Simon (1974, pp. 109–110) note:

> Women on children's and family TV programs are consistently portrayed as being concerned with appearances: their own, their family's, and their home's. These women never appear to occupy positions of authority either at home or on the job; and the overall image is the traditional one that women are dependent, and perform expressive and socio-emotional roles within a family context.

Gerbner (1972, p. 45) notes:

> Women typically represent romantic or family interest, close human contact, love. Males can act in nearly any role. . . . While only one in three male leads in the programs surveyed was shown as intending to or ever having been married, two of every three females were married or expected to marry in the story.

By categorizing the division of labor in society and in the home, and the division of social and familial power, by sex, Busby (1975, p. 113) found that males dominated in the home as well as in society in general.

Research concerning television images of the family is a neglected area. There is an abundance of literature in the social sciences related to the family, and considerable research has been conducted on the American family (see Wakefield, Allen, and Washchuck [1979]). But the study of family images on television needs more in-depth examination. Since family-content studies have been restricted to prime-time and other programs not specifically directed at children, children's television programming, in particular, should be analyzed for information about family portrayals. It is hoped that this study will help to fill that gap.

17 RECOGNITION OF FAMILY AND KINSHIP RELATIONS

Twelve out of the 235 program segments studied dealt with domestic relations (marriage, the home, and family affairs) as a major subject area. In addition, 21 others dealt with domestic relations as minor or subordinate subject matter. Thus, of all segments coded, about 14 percent dealt in some meaningful way with the subject of the family and home. Also, when asked to "flag" any segments which in any way referred to or portrayed any type of family or kinship unit, coders noted 94 (40 percent) of the segments as "relevant" to family relations.

These are only crude measures of the extent to which family and kinship patterns are dealt with in the programs, because in some cases the portrayal or reference was incidental or almost irrelevant to the story itself. Therefore, in this chapter, we will analyze the distribution of various family and kinship units, by looking in detail at the family structures, the program formats in which they appeared, and how important they were in the programs.

FAMILY STRUCTURES

Overall, there were 110 family-kinship units coded in the 94 program segments flagged as relevant to family relations.* Only 46 of

*Four additional references are not included here because they involved only a passing reference to families. For example, an "In the News" episode reported a story about an integration court fight in which parents didn't want their daughters bussed to an all-black school. Another involved a mouse who talked a lion out of eating him when he said, "I have a wife and kids at home." A third featured a boy who had taken over as night watchman for his father, and the fourth involved a short segment of "Hot Fudge" in which a boy talks of his mother's not letting him have a motorcycle.

these were coded as "central" to the program. Interestingly, the most frequent family structure found was the single-parent family, accounting for one-third of all units. Twice as many male single-parent units were found (22.7 percent of the total) as female single-parent units (10.9 percent). These were followed by nuclear families that included father, mother, and one or more children (29.1 percent); children-only units (siblings without parents—12.7 percent); and married couples (10.9 percent). The remainder were scattered in nine other kinship classes (see Table 17.1).

Importance of Family Units in the Programs

Each family-kinship unit (F-K unit) was coded for importance in the segment as follows:

1. Irrelevant—a family kinship unit is depicted, but there is little or no interaction between kinship characters and the story does not involve family situation, conflict, or cooperation.
2. Incidental—kinship characters are shown and interact, but the plot is not related to family topics, conflicts, or issues.
3. Central— characters are related and interact frequently and/or the major plot or topic revolves around a family unit in some way.

Table 17.1   Types of Family-Kinship Units in the Programs

FAMILY STRUCTURE/ KINSHIP UNITS	TOTAL UNITS		UNITS CENTRAL TO STORY	
	NUMBER	PERCENT	NUMBER	PERCENT
Nuclear family	32	29.1	22	69
Extended family	2	1.8	2	100
Single parent (female)	12	10.9	5	42
Single parent (male)	25	22.7	6	24
Married couple	12	10.9	6	50
Children only	14	12.7	3	21
Aunt-nephew	2	1.8	—	0
Aunt-niece	—	—	—	—
Uncle-nephew	7	6.4	2	29
Uncle-niece	1	0.9	—	0
Cousins	1	0.9	—	0
Grandmother-granddaughter	1	0.9	—	0
Grandmother-grandson	1	0.9	—	0
Grandfather-granddaughter	—	—	—	—
Grandfather-grandson	—	—	—	—
Total	110	99.9*	46	42

*Due to rounding error.

The segments most likely to offer direct lessons for the child viewer are those in category 3, in which major emphasis is placed on family issues, interactions, conflicts, or problem solving. Overall, 46 of the 110 F-K units (42 percent) were classifed as central, although this varied considerably by type of family structure (see Table 17.2).* Whereas 70 percent of nuclear families and 50 percent of married couples were central to the programs, less than 30 percent of all (male and female combined) single-parent families were, and even smaller proportions of other kinship units were central to the programs.

In addition, five out of 12 female single-parent units were central, whereas only six out of 25 male single-parent units were. Female single parents were thus about twice as likely to be involved in family-relation situations as were male single parents.

Family Structure and Nature of Family Relationships

Each F-K unit was coded according to the nature of the relationship —either close, neutral, or distant.* Most nuclear-family or single-parent family relationships were judged to be close (i.e., affectionate, helping, and friendly), as shown in Table 17.3. Married couples, children, and other kinship units were more often neutral or distant in their relationships.

Table 17.2 Family Structure, by Importance in the Segments

FAMILY STRUCTURE	IMPORTANCE (NUMBER OF F-K UNITS)				PERCENT CENTRAL TO PROGRAMS
	IRRELEVANT	INCIDENTAL	CENTRAL	TOTAL	
Nuclear and extended	2	8	24	34	70.6
Single parent (female)	5	2	5	12	41.7
Single parent (male)	7	12	6	25	24.0
Married couple	3	3	6	12	50.0
Children only	5	6	3	14	21.4
All other	4	7	2	13	15.4
Total	26	38	46	110	41.8

---

*Because of the small number in some kinship groups, the family-structure categories are collapsed into six groups.

---

*Changing relationships moving from distant to close during the story were coded as close and vice versa.

Table 17.3   Family Structure, by Nature of the Relationship

FAMILY STRUCTURE	CLOSE	NEUTRAL	DISTANT	NA*	TOTALS	PERCENT CLOSE
Nuclear and extended	25	3	4	2	34	74
Single female parent	9	1	2	—	12	75
Single male parent	19	1	4	1	25	76
Married couple	6	3	2	1	12	50
Children only	8	1	4	1	14	57
All other	5	5	2	1	13	38
Total	72	14	18	6	110	65

*Not coded because of lack of information.

Family Structures in Various Program Formats

When compared with the percentage of all segments studied (235), F-K Units appeared somewhat less frequently in comedy and information programs than in action/adventure ones. That is, cartoon comedies and other comedy dramas accounted for 50% of all segments and 48 percent of F-K units; for action/ adventure and other dramas, the figures were 19 percent and 31 percent, respectively; and for informational programs, 29 percent and 21 percent.

Certain groups, however, seem more likely to appear in comedy programs—nine of twelve married couples (75 percent), and 11 of 12 other kinship groups (85 percent);* data are in Table 17.4.

When F-K units appear in information programs, they are more often central to the program. Thus, 13 of 23 F-K units in information programs (57 percent) were classified as central, whereas only 18 of 53 (34 percent) were so classed in comedy dramas (see Table 17.5).

The above figures provide a general overview of the distribution of F-K units in the sample. The next chapter will deal with parental roles and functions within the family.

---

*Familiar examples are Daffy Duck and nephew, Speedy Gonzales and nephew, Scooby and Scrappy Doo, Top Cat and nephew, Popeye and nephews, and cousins Maynard and Sheepdog.

Table 17.4 Family Structure and Program Format

FAMILY STRUCTURE	NUMBER OF F-K UNITS IN PROGRAMS				PERCENT IN CARTOON COMEDIES AND OTHER COMEDY DRAMAS
	CARTOON COMEDIES AND OTHER COMEDY DRAMAS	ACTION/ ADVENTURE AND OTHER DRAMAS	INFORMATIONAL PROGRAMS	TOTAL	
Nuclear and extended	15	11	8	34	44
Single parent	14	15	8	37	38
Married couple	9	—	3	12	75
Children only	4	6	4	14	28
Other kinship groups	11	2	—	13	85
Total	53	34	23	110	48
Percent by format	48%	31%	21%	100.0	
Percent of all segments studied	50%	19%	29%	98%*	

*Remaining 2 percent were variety and other entertainment segments, which contained no F-K units.

135

Table 17.5   Format, by Importance in the Segments

FORMAT	IMPORTANCE OF UNITS				PERCENT
	IRRELEVANT	INCIDENTAL	CENTRAL	TOTAL	CENTRAL
Cartoon comedies and other comedy dramas	14	21	18	53	34
Action/adventure and other dramas	6	13	15	34	44
Informational programs	6	4	13	23	57
Total	26	38	46	110	42

18 PARENTAL ROLES AND FUNCTIONS

In numbers, males outnumber females in almost all family and kinship roles for all characters: of 263 characters identified by family role, 62 percent were males. This was true for all family-kinship roles except for grandparents, since there were three grandmothers and only one grandfather (see Table 18.1).

Female characters, however, were more likely to be in family than in nonfamily roles. That is, overall, females comprised only 22 percent of all characters in all program segments. In segments which were not relevant to F-K units, they comprised only 17 percent, whereas in the segments dealing with family and kinship relations, they numbered 38 percent of all characters.

The purpose of this chapter is to analyze parental activities, dominance patterns, and other parental characteristics in those segments in which parent roles were portrayed.

DOMINANCE PATTERNS

In single-parent family units, the parent acted as the dominant member of the family, whether a single male or a single female parent. The one exception was a story of a mother-son relationship in which the mother appeared to have no control over her son, who was rated dominant.

If only married couples were depicted (12 such units), the husband was rated as dominant in five and the wife in two. They were rated as equal in the remaining five units.

When both mother and father are present in nuclear- and extended-family units, most frequently the father serves in the traditional role of

Table 18.1 Sex Distributions, by Family Role

| | NUMBER | | | PERCENT |
FAMILY ROLE	MALES	FEMALES	TOTAL	MALE
Parents	54	39	93	58
Children	66	35	101	65
Spouses	14	11	25	56
Siblings	10	6	16	62
Grandparents	1	3	4	25
Uncles, aunts	7	3	10	70
Nephew, nieces	9	2	11	82
Cousins	2	1	3	67
Total	163	100	263	62
Nonfamily roles	701	143	844	83
Total	864	243	1107	78

Note: The numbers in this table cannot be equated with numbers of family-kinship units in Table 17.1. Here we are counting identifications of individuals (who may appear alone) as to family roles. The F-K unit figures refer to relationships between two or more family or kinship individuals.

head of the family. Out of 34 such units, the father dominated in 17 and the mother in only two. In seven, they were rated as equal. In several cases, however, even though there was a nuclear-family unit, the interactions were primarily those of husband-wife rather than parental relationships. In such cases, the wife was frequently the dominant one. This is shown in Table 18.2, in which three mothers acting in the wife role dominated the husband, whereas, conversely, only two fathers acting in the husband role were dominant.

Some examples will illustrate how these dominance patterns emerge in children's television. Although the Flintstones are usually shown as a nuclear family, the interaction patterns and conflicts were generally between Fred and Wilma and did not involve their children— that is, they were shown more as husband-wife than as parents. In these stories, the balance of power shifts between them. Although Fred often seems able to do what he wants while Wilma takes care of the house, in the end, Wilma often uncovers Fred's foibles. In several episodes they were rated as equal partners.

In the traditional family programs such as "Leave It to Beaver" or "The Brady Bunch," the father is the one usually called upon to resolve family conflicts and mete out any discipline necessary.

In the informational treatment of family relations, the father is often not only shown as the dominant member, but also the source of a number of problems because of his dominance. This was true in segments of "Kids are People Too" and "30 Minutes" that dealt with abused

Table 18.2 Dominance Patterns in Nuclear and Extended Families

DOMINANT FAMILY MEMBER	NUMBER	PERCENT
Father in father role	17	50.0
Mother in mother role	2	5.9
Father in husband role	2	5.9
Mother in wife role	3	8.8
Equal	7	20.6
Uncertain dominance	3	8.8
Total	34	100.0

teenagers and runaway children, and in which the father was identified as the abuser or the unreasonable parent.

In stories of adventure, the father is almost always the dominant member, who thinks clearly, gives orders, and performs heroic deeds. We found such examples in families in "Valley of the Dinosaurs," "The Lone Ranger," and "Starblazers."

Female dominance occurred only in cartoon comedies. In a "Yogi Bear" cartoon, the mother took the initiative in protecting her baby while the father seemed unconcerned. This was also true in the episodes in which the wife dominated the husband. These portray the stereotype of the henpecked and timid husband. For example, in a "Daffy Duck" cartoon, Daffy is cast as a fearful and submissive husband who is bossed around by a domineering wife. Another example was found in the short segment of "Dough-nuts" in which Henry Dimble was so timid, meek, and mild that he was not only afraid of his wife, but also of offending the sales clerk who sold him a present he did not want.

Equality in marriage was demonstrated in the programs of "¿Qué Pasa USA?" showing a newly married Catholic woman and a Jewish man; and in "The Fat Albert Show," in which the child was reassured by his parents about "the new baby."

Heavy discipline by strict parents does not seem to be the common pattern in the programs studied. However, the male parent was judged to be stern in his parental role much more often than was the female parent (see Table 18.3).

Table 18.3 Was the Character Portrayed as the Stern Parent?

RESPONSE	FATHER	PERCENT	MOTHER	PERCENT
Yes	15	25.4	7	15.2
No	39	66.1	35	76.1
Unidentifiable	5	8.5	4	8.7
Total	59	100.0	46	100.0

In summary, when parental roles were depicted on children's TV, the father (as father) was dominant in two-thirds of the cases, the mother (as mother) in one-fifth, and they were equal partners in about one-tenth. If children do learn family-role expectations from children's television, there is little question as to who is supposed to be boss in the family.

PARENTAL ACTIVITIES

Other role expectations may be learned by observing the type of activities engaged in by parent figures. Fathers and husbands are more likely to be engaged in work and adventurous activities than are mothers and wives. Women are most concerned with daily living activities—primarily homemaking duties (see Table 18.4).

In work activities the father and the husband are shown either at work (e.g., getting a contract and shearing sheep) or as the family provider (coming home from work). Leisure activities include vacationing, visiting neighbors, camping, working on hobbies, and going to a dinner party, on a tour or on a picnic. Daily living includes taking care of the baby, advising children, cooking, cleaning, etc.

Although mothers may be presented in adventure stories, the action usually involves the father's appearance with sons in programs of adventure. This is true in the program "Thunderbirds," in which two sons are trapped in a mine and father helps in their rescue. The other family unit in the program consists of a father and three sons who make up the rescue team. Similarly, Dr. Quest and son Johnny Quest engage in deep-sea adventures in the Caribbean. In another episode they are attacked by a sea monster when rescuing a ship laden with gold. On "Force Five," involving both a son and daughter, Dr. Copernicus risks his life in saving his son Joey from the jet robot of the Pandemonium Empire.

The sole father-daughter program was of a different nature. This was on the "Heathcliff and Dingbat" animated comedy about the King's

Table 18.4   Primary Activities of Male and Female Family Members

TYPE OF ACTIVITY	NUMBER		NUMBER		
	FATHERS	MOTHERS	HUSBANDS	WIVES	TOTAL
Work	13	1	1	1	16
Adventure	5	3	3	1	12
Leisure	9	9	5	4	27
Daily living	12	21	1	2	36
Other, miscellaneous	13	6	2	3	24
Uncertain, unclassifiable	7	6	—	—	13
Total	59	46	12	12	129

daughter, Fair Maiden, who had been kidnapped by Sir Grimacelot. The King hired Dingbat and the Creeps to rescue her.

Parental Incompetence

Both mothers and fathers were rated as to competency (see Table 18.5). Fathers seem much more apt to be portrayed as incompetent— either in parental duties or other aspects of their life—than mothers.

Although the general pattern is that of parental competency for fathers, husbands, mothers, and wives, the inept father is sometimes singled out as the basis for humor. One form of incompetence is shown in the lazy or irresponsible father. Examples are the father cat who relaxes and makes his son catch the mice, the father panda who is too busy reading the racing form to answer his child's question, or the father who fails to look after his child while watching TV.

Another type is the clumsy father who can't keep his child quiet or can't catch a woodpecker. In "The Flintstones," both Fred and Barney are often shown as incompetent in episodes dealing with camping (being afraid of animals), or with building a house (falling off a ladder into cement mix).

When asked to explain ratings of a father's incompetence, the words used by coders to describe fathers provide the flavor of the inept-father image often used for comedy purposes: "obstinate," "stubborn," "lazy," "clumsy," "well intentioned," and "irresponsible." Although generally humorous, parental incompetence was sometimes shown as leading to serious problems in those programs addressed to child abuse and runaway children.

Traditional and Nontraditional Parents

It is not simple to define in detail the traditional and the nontraditional family. As we have seen so far, however, most family portrayals tend to be traditional in the sense of the father's dominant position in the family, and the patterns of work and domestic activities of the par-

Table 18.5 Competency of Mother and Father

RATING	FATHERS		MOTHERS	
	NUMBER	PERCENT	NUMBER	PERCENT
Competent	35	59.3	34	73.9
Incompetent	17	28.8	6	13.0
Unclassifiable	7	11.9	6	13.1
Total	59	100.0	46	100.0

ents. Supporting these images are judgments of coders as to whether mother and father roles were traditional or nontraditional (see Table 18.6).

In addition, the characters were judged as to whether they were nurturing, assumed here to be a traditional female family role. Because of child-care duties primarily, mothers were judged more nurturing than fathers. However, a considerable number of fathers were also judged to demonstrate this trait (see Table 18.7).

Nontraditional fathers were judged to be so by the coders primarily on the basis of relationships with their children. Although still maintaining their role as household head, several fathers were described as nontraditional because of the ease with which they displayed affection, and concern over the welfare of their children. This is closely related to the nurturing variable.

Because these variables of traditional/nontraditional and nurturing behaviors were not well-enough defined in the study, they are not considered statistically reliable indices. They are discussed here primarily to illustrate types of behavior that might later be refined into more reliable measures. Some of the examples are interesting, however: They include the father bulldog who cares for, hugs, kisses, and sleeps with his arm around his young son; a father in "The Thunderbirds" who talks about how important his sons are to him and how he wishes to spend more time with them; a father who talks to his son about the arrival of the new baby and the facts of life; the father in "The Brady Bunch"; and Plasticman, who takes Baby Plas along and teaches him how to help capture the criminal.

Table 18.6 Traditional and Nontraditional Family Roles

ROLE	FATHER	MOTHER	HUSBAND	WIFE
Traditional	31	31	5	5
Nontraditional	9	8	5	5
Unclassifiable	19	7	2	2
Total	59	46	12	12

Table 18.7 Nurturing and Parental Role

WAS CHARACTER NURTURING?	FATHERS		MOTHERS	
	NUMBER	PERCENT	NUMBER	PERCENT
Yes	21	35.6	23	50.0
No	29	49.2	17	37.0
Unclassifiable	9	15.2	6	13.0
Total	59	100.0	46	100.0

Although one might expect that single-female-parent family units would be less traditional, this did not seem to be the case. The only examples are in two episodes of "The Partridge Family" in which the mother is portrayed as part of the musical family group and as a nontraditional-mother model.

Summary

In family-related children's programs, male and female parental-role portrayals tend to reinforce the traditional view of family relations with respect to male dominance and female nurturing. They also reinforce the traditional patterns of male work and adventure and female domestic activities. In addition, there is perpetuated the myth of the lazy, clumsy, and incompetent father.

There are some exceptions to these tendencies noted, however. A significant number of fathers and husbands were portrayed in nurturing roles in relation to their children. The examples found show this to be nearly always a same-sex, father-son relationship.

Although the single-parent family unit cannot be described as the traditional family unit, the parental behaviors exhibited in these units could well be described as traditional.

19 FAMILY PORTRAYALS: PROBLEMS AND CONFLICTS

Several aspects of family interactions were explored in this study. Answers were sought to such questions as the following: What family-related conflicts or other situations were portrayed or discussed? These include such topics as divorce or separation, sibling rivalry, extramarital affairs, and discipline. How were conflict situations resolved, and who in the family unit contributed most to their resolution? What kinds of functions are performed by parents or the family in child training or socialization? Here, we are looking for portrayals dealing with teaching the child manners, responsibility, independence, self-image, and other areas dealing with the family function of socialization of the child.

The answers to these questions were sought not in quantitative terms, but, rather, by closely examining the plots, subject matter, and family-conflict situations of the programs to provide examples available to the child viewer, (see Appendix C for short summaries of program segments). Discussed here are examples from dramatic episodes or informational segments in which family situations are a major part of the program. Other minor or incidental portrayals are not considered relevant enough for detailed treatment because of the lack of interaction between or among members of the family unit.*

---

*Examples of these not discussed in detail are the married couple on "Gilligan's Island"; Commissioner Gordon and his daughter (Batgirl) on an episode of "Batman"; mother holding daughter's hand ("Schoolhouse Rock"); family groups in "Attack of the Killer Bees"; and two episodes of "Plasticman and Baby Plas." In these and others there was little or no interaction among family members.

PARENT—CHILD CONFLICT

In various family-related program segments, the conflict between parent and child was the most frequent single theme. The source of the conflict varied considerably, however.

The most serious treatments were found in informational programs dealing with such topics as child abuse, runaway children, and unreasonable parents. The less serious situations usually involved some sort of child disobedience and occurred in cartoons and in other comedy dramas.

Child Abuse and Runaway Children

In the segment "Abused Teenagers," on "30 Minutes," the focus was on a teenager who started a self-help group. This program explored in some detail, through interviews with parents and teens, the background of the father involved and the help he received through Parents Anonymous. It is a success story in which the father now supports the work of his daughter's teen self-help group.

A short segment of "Kids Are People Too" dealt with the problem of runaways. The children themselves are interviewed and tell of reasons for running away—an abusive father, parental pressures to do well in school, and an inability to communicate with parents.

"For Kids Only" presented a panel discussion among young people who were interviewed by counsellors from Place Runaway House. One of the children discussed his problem with his father and his own problem with drugs. Another received help at Place Runaway House and reported better parent-child relationships through talking things out with parents.

One segment dealt with the potential of running away from home in the program "Leave It to Beaver." After being disciplined (his father took away his car keys), a friend of the Cleavers' son decides to run away to join the merchant marine. After some misunderstandings and interaction with Mr. Cleaver, the boy overhears his father's concern for him and aborts his own plans.

Discipline Problems

Many of the problems of discipline did not involve serious breaches, but sometimes led to dangers for the offspring. Many were in the humorous context of a cartoon comedy. The father was usually the one who was involved in dealing with discipline problems. In one instance, when Sylvester the Cat's son Junior refused to eat his porridge, his father dumped the bowl on his head. When Wally Cleaver is late, he is scolded by his father.

Mother's discipline was often related to the welfare of the child. The mother of Baby Huey told him to come down from a roof "before you catch your death of cold," as did the mother hen who took her child out of the rain for the same reason after he wandered off.

Somewhat more serious situations arose when a daughter and a son in "Valley of the Dinosaurs" disobeyed instructions and stayed in the cave. And Davey's father lectured his son when he behaved irresponsibly in a "Davey and Goliath" episode.

Other Parent-Child Problems

In the short segment "Dear Alex and Annie," a 14-year-old girl wrote a letter in which she stated her embarrassment over her mother's pregnancy; and in one segment of "So the Story Goes," a strict and possessive father forbade his daughter to marry her true love, kept her a prisoner, and arranged a marriage with a nobleman.

Parental Conflict

Parental conflict in children's television usually does not include other members of the family. This is revealing because real-life parental conflict often does involve children in the family. The topic of parental conflict and its ramifications for the child was found in only one brief segment of the program "For Kids Only," in which a young black boy wrote to "Dear Barbara" about his parents, who fought all the time both before and after their divorce. He had developed a negative view of marriage, saying that "marriage stinks" and that he would stay "single forever." He was advised to learn from his parents' experience and not close himself off from the possiblity of marriage.

Husband-Wife Conflict

Family situations in nuclear-family units often do not involve the family as a whole, but only the parents. The children are, if anything, only observers or background scenery. They are husband-wife conflicts more than family-interaction situations. The source of conflict, in other words, is between married partners, not in the family unit as a whole. "The Flintstones" series and other dramas provide several examples of husband-wife conflict relating to various themes.

Several episodes related to messages about sex roles in marriage. One example is a Flintstone camping trip on which the men didn't want their wives to go because "it's not the sort of thing for a woman." Another is provided by Daffy Duck, a very henpecked husband, whose male ego is threatened when he is ordered to sit on an egg. He says that it is "sissy stuff" and "sickening how women make such a big deal out of motherhood."

Extramarital affairs are another example of husband-wife conflict. This theme occurred in both a "Jetson's" and a "Flintstones" episode, and in another "Daffy Duck" cartoon, in which Daffy chased after the wife of a rooster.

A third type of husband-wife conflict—in-law problems—occurred in a "Flintstones" episode involving a planned visit by Fred Flintstone's mother-in-law. Childish husbands are cause for further conflict in which angry wives must lecture and punish husbands for childish behavior.

Sibling Relations

In programs in which siblings were portrayed without parents, there were conflicts in which the older brother was often the dominant one. This was true for the big-brother/little-sister and big-brother/little-brother units in "The New Fat Albert Show." Both used physical force to make the younger sibling obey and return home. In "The Great Pussycat Chase," the brother saved his sister's life when she was hanging on the side of a tall building; and in a segment of "Way to Go," two brothers help their sister, who is looking for her grandmother.

Twin siblings are well represented in the programs; five sets of twins were found. These include the twin brothers Droopy and Drippy who interact very little in a "Tom and Jerry" cartoon; Pixie and Dixie in cartoon hijinks with a cat; and the twin (ghost) brothers Dunk and Dink on "Goober and the Ghost Chasers." The Wonder Twins work in harmony with each other in "The Invasion of the Brain Creatures," and two older brothers act as brothers-in-crime, attempting to unfairly gain land and start a cattle-rustling operation in "The Lone Ranger."

Sibling rivalry was treated in some depth in only one program, "The New Fat Albert Show," in a segment on "Little Brothers and Sisters." Dum Donald, whose parents are expecting a new baby, is upset at the prospect, but, after its arrival, is quite pleased. The situation leads to an interesting discussion, in which the father tells his son the facts of life and reassures him of their love for him.

Another example occurs in "Leave It to Beaver," in which Wally is angry with Beaver for telling others he might join the merchant marine, but gets over it when his father points out how it has helped him with his girlfriend. In "The Brady Bunch," jealousy arises among the children of the two widowed parents, who are being married. The problem is not discussed directly but is resolved anyway. And in "Starblazers," one brother is jealous of another for the attention he is receiving after having graduated from the Space Academy. This is resolved when the mother talks with the son.

Other Kinship Relations

When uncles are involved it is most likely an uncle-nephew relationship (seven units) and less often an uncle-niece one. Moreover, the plots are quite similar and can be described as the protective-uncle/ mischievous-nephew relationship. This was true for six of the seven units, including three episodes that involved Scooby and Scrappy Doo, Speedy Gonzales and his nephew, Daffy Duck and his nephew, and Popeye and his nephews. Nephews are frightened by a witch; are playing with fireworks; and chased by animals, a circus strongman, and a caveman.

Two nieces must deal with an uncle in the cartoon "Foggy Doggy." Here, the uncle is miserly, mean, nervous, and clumsy, and his nieces do their best to please him.

Aunt Jessica (alias Spiderwoman) and Aunt Quinn both participate in adventures with their nephews in the Amazon and on "Storm Island." Both seem competent and caring aunts.

The cousins identified in this study were Maynard and Sheepdog in "Gigglesnort Hotel." They interact little. One grandmother is Little Red Riding Hood's; another appears with her grandson in the "Heathcliff and Dingbat Show" dealing with a burglar.

Mixed Marriage

If not conflict, there was considerable concern and discussion of the recent marriage of a young Cuban woman and her Jewish-American husband in "¿Qué Pasa USA?" In this extended family, there was a good deal of difficulty in accepting the marriage, especially for the grandmother, who tried to persuade the new husband to convert his religion. After much discussion and observation of the obviously happy union, the family gradually accepted the marriage, especially when it was announced that the young wife was pregnant. The pair are portrayed as an extremely happy couple who are equal partners in marriage.

Family Support and Cooperation

Not all situations depicted involved family conflict. In many cases the family worked together in solving problems—usually those imposed from outside the family unit. According to family sociologists, one important function of the family lies in the social support that is afforded members of the family unit.

Supporting relationships are often demonstrated in the program "Barbapapa." Three separate segments demonstrated family help and support. First, they work as a family in shearing sheep, and when the son has a new idea for doing it faster, he is encouraged by his father to always try new ideas. When there is a mishap and the son is accidentally sheared of his fur by his father, he is comforted by his mother and helped by his brother, who weaves his fur back into a coat for him until his own can grow back. In another case, the family encourages son Barba Bo as he is learning pottery and sculpture.

Related to the social-support function is the function served by the family as protector. In a "Yogi Bear" episode, the mother shows great concern in protecting her baby. And in a somewhat unusual situation, a father bulldog nurtures and protects his son from a cat. He becomes very aggressive and protective when he thinks the son is in danger, and also kisses and hugs him and sleeps with his arm around him.

Child Training and Development

As alluded to in many of the previous examples, the family functions in the socialization of the child—primarily by parental advice or counseling. Some program segments dealt directly with advice giving: "Dear Alex and Annie" and "Dear Barbara"; with discussions of family problems: "For Kids Only," "Kids Are People Too," and "30 Minutes"; or with prosocial family drama: "Davey and Goliath" and "The New Fat Albert Show." Other socializing messages are embedded in comedy dramas and other dramatic segments, whether intentionally or unintentionally.

The understanding of parental behaviors was discussed directly in those programs dealing with child abuse, runaways, and parent-child difficulties in communication.

The dramatic segments also provide advice to the child audience but not directly. Rather, it is given to the children of the family in the stories. This is most obvious in "Little Brothers and Sisters," in which the father explains to his son where babies come from, consoles him, and builds his confidence by telling him what a good son he is. It is also significant in "Davey and Goliath" when the father tells Davey about responsibility and freedom. In another episode, Davey's mother shows interest in her son's newspaper and teaches him independence by not giving him a direct answer to a question about how to thank the editor he is working for.

Beyond these prosocial dramas, different lessons were imparted to the children—often by the mother. For example, mothers advised children to go to bed and get out of the rain to protect their health. Another teaches her son not to sulk, by telling him to look in the mirror at him-self. And another grooms her children and tells them to look nice and be kind to their guests.

The father's role is somewhat mixed. Positive lessons are provided by one father in "The Lone Ranger," who cautions a child to be careful. He has also taught the daughter how to swim "real good."

The kindly uncle is sometimes a source of child learning. Daffy Duck states that he tried to steer his nephew right and taught him not to be distrustful of everyone. And Uncle Popeye warns his nephews of the dangers of fireworks.

In several cases, however, the father is unresponsive or negative to-ward his child. One son does all the work while his father, who has cau-tioned him against lying down on the job, nevertheless relaxes and takes advantage of his son. In another instance, the father (reading the racing form) tells his son not to bother him because he's busy. Aggres-sive behavior is encouraged by one bulldog father who wants his son to chew on the cat's tail. Finally, the father who takes his noisy son to the movies tries to keep him quiet by shushing him, then becomes angry and takes a swing at him; the son runs away.

20 SUMMARY: PORTRAYALS OF FAMILIES

The major rationale for this study of family and kinship relations on children's television was to discover and describe patterns and tendencies in the portrayals. It has been done with the assumption that such content provides the child viewer with information about family roles and structures that he or she may learn and use as models.

In this analysis, several aspects of family relationships were shown providing both positive and negative messages for young children. Some of these messages are conveyed implicitly through the frequencies and types of family units portrayed. Some are conveyed directly through informational and prosocial dramatic programs. Others are conveyed indirectly through parental and other family roles in cartoons and animated adventure programs.

About four out of ten program segments were relevant in some way to family or kinship relations. Two out of ten dealt in some significant way with family relationships, and about one in ten dealt with the nuclear family.

Single-parent families are considerably overrepresented in children's television as compared to estimates for the real population. This is especially true for single-male-parent family units, which outnumber single-female-parent units by two to one—unlike the proportions in the U.S. population, where single female parents vastly outnumber single-male-parent families.

The child seldom has an opportunity to see the extended family unit; uncles are considerably more numerous than aunts; and grandparents and older people in general are seldom portrayed. The child viewer may also see more males than females in both family and nonfamily relationships, although females are more apt to appear in the family context than not.

What the child does see are traditional family roles in which the father is rather stern, dominant, and often engaged in work and adventure activities. He is also the one most responsible for discipline in the family. In addition, he is often portrayed as somewhat incompetent and less nurturing than the mother. The mother, on the other hand, is more competent in her role, engages in household and daily living activities, and is more nurturing.

Available for the child viewer are frequent examples of close relationships between father and son, especially in adventure and action settings—much more frequent than mother-daughter or father-daughter relationships.

The child viewer is also exposed to a variety of family and marital conflicts. Parent-child conflicts deal with disobedience and discipline problems. Informational programs dealing with child abuse and runaway children offer examples of prosocial messages of hope for those involved.

Frequently, the child is introduced to the marital problems of parents or of married couples without children. Seldom do these conflicts involve the child, however, as is frequently the case in the life of the child viewer. Husband-wife conflicts occur over definition of sex roles, extramarital affairs, in-law problems, and childish behaviors by husbands.

In sibling conflict, the older brother is usually the one who is responsible for resolution of the conflict.

The child viewer may also witness a good deal of family support and cooperation in addition to the conflicts noted above. Family relations are most often shown as close and cooperative, confirming previous research on family interaction patterns.

A number of examples of positive child-development messages were found in the stories dealing with sibling relations and parental guidance and the teaching of responsibility. These lessons come both from parents and from kindly uncles. Sometimes failing in his responsibilities, however, is the father.

Overall, the family on children's television is portrayed in a traditional and stereotyped manner, with parental roles being clearly defined and children having little say or power in family decision making. Although some of the changes in family structures seem to be reflected in the programming—e.g., to the single-parent family—it is not a very accurate reflection. In addition, many familial problem areas—financial difficulties, divorce, aging members of the family, and troubles in school, for example—are absent.

In terms of family-development patterns, most nuclear families consist of schoolage or teenage children and the parents, whereas young childbearing families and those with preschool children, those that provide launching centers, or those with aging family members are much underrepresented.

It is somewhat difficult to make definitive judgments about the adequacy or the frequency of portrayals of the family on children's television. Is, for example, the lazy or irresponsible father, who has difficulty driving a nail without hitting his thumb, more real than the perfect father, who, asking his son to mow the lawn, gets the quick and eager response, "right away, Dad"?

Overall, the family portrayals represented in this study provide a mixed picture. Although serious treatment of a number of family-related problems is provided in the context of informational and prosocial drama, many simplistic cartoon-comedy and adventure programs provide stereotyped and negative messages for the child viewer.

For the reader who may wish to utilize the categories of analysis that appear in this study, Appendix A lists the categories and instructions used in coding each character ("Character Codes"), and includes the coding forms that accompany the study ("Character Code Sheet" and "Family Relationship Sheet").

Appendix A Character Codes

Column Number	Variable Number	Variable Name, Codes, Instructions
		SEGMENT TITLE: (write in)
		CHARACTER NAME: (write in) If no name, write in identifying description.
		ROLE IN THE STORY: (write in)
1-3	01	SEGMENT NO.: (Copy from Program Segment Form)
4	02	CHARACTER NUMBER: (1-9)
5	03	SEX:
		1 — male (or character with male voice, dress, etc.)
		2 — female (or character with female voice, dress, etc.)
		9 — uncertain (animals, robots, etc., with no cues)
6	04	AGE GROUP:
		1 — child
		2 — teen
		3 — young adult (approx. 20-35)
		4 — middle age (approx. 35-65)
		5 — elderly
		9 — uncertain (animals, robots, etc.)
7	05	RACE:
		1 — white
		2 — black

Column Number	Variable Number	Variable Name, Codes, Instructions
		3 — other race (humans)
		4 — animals
		5 — other-nonhuman
		9 — uncertain
8	06	SOCIAL CLASS:
		1 — elite (upper-upper, royalty, etc.)
		2 — upper class (wealthy)
		3 — upper-middle (professional job, i.e., talk show host)
		4 — lower-middle
		5 — lower class
		6 — déclassé (hoboes, criminals, others outside class structure)
		9 — uncertain (animals, others without human class characteristics)
9–10	07	ETHNICITY:
		01 — African/Afro-American
		02 — American Indian
		03 — Anglo-Saxon/Nordic
		04 — Arab, Egyptian
		05 — Asian/Oriental
		06 — Jewish
		07 — Latin, Caribbean
		08 — Greek, Turkish, Mediterranean
		09 — Mexican
		10 — Puerto Rican
		11 — Russian
		12 — Slavic
		13 — Germanic
		14 — French
		15 — Italian
		19 — Other (explain in notes)
		99 — Uncertain or not applicable
11	08	MARITAL STATUS:
		1 — Single, unattached individual
		2 — Married
		3 — Divorced
		4 — Widowed
		5 — Not applicable (children, teens, animals)
		9 — Uncertain

Column Number	Variable Number	Variable Name, Codes, Instructions
12	09	CITIZENSHIP: 1 — U.S. 2 — Foreign 3 — Uncertain
13	10	IS CHARACTER EMPLOYED? 0 — no, or uncertain 1 — yes
—	—	(WRITE IN OCCUPATION)
14–15	11	OCCUPATION: (see separate code sheet for occupations)
16	12	IS OCCUPATION CENTRAL OR INCIDENTAL TO CHARACTER'S ROLE IN THE STORY: (e.g., superheroes with secret identity, etc.) 0 — no occupation 1 — central 2 — incidental
—	—	STORY ROLE TYPE: (Write in: e.g., "superhero," "sidekick," etc.)
17–18	13	STORY ROLE TYPE CODES: (see separate code sheet)
19	14	DRAMATIC ROLE: 1 — hero or comic hero 2 — villain or comic villain 3 — other major character—central to plot 4 — submajor character—helpers 5 — minor character
20–21	15	FAMILY ROLE: 00 — none 01 — mother 02 — father 03 — son 04 — daughter 05 — grandmother 06 — grandfather 07 — husband (no-child family) 08 — wife (no-child family) 09 — stepmother 10 — stepfather 11 — stepson 12 — stepdaughter

Column Number	Variable Number	Variable Name, Codes, Instructions
		13 — adopted son
		14 — adopted daughter
		15 — brother (no-parent family)
		16 — sister (no-parent family)
		17 — aunt
		18 — uncle
		19 — niece
		20 — nephew
		21 — cousin
		29 — other (guardian, ward, etc.)
		99 — uncertain
—	—	SEX-ROLE ATTRIBUTES: (code "0" for none; "1" for some; "2" for much) (Explain under notes).
22	16	AGGRESSION: (rough-and-tumble play, physical fighting, often antisocial, violent behaviors, verbal threat)
23	17	ACTIVITY: (active play, outdoor play, difficulty sitting still)
24	18	CURIOSITY AND EXPLORATORY BEHAVIOR: (finding out how things work, exploring activities).
25	19	IMPULSIVITY: (difficulty resisting temptation, easily distracted, often resulting in getting into dangerous situations or taking chances).
26	20	ANXIETY: (being afraid of things, sometimes manifested in more compliance, obedience).
27	21	IMPORTANCE OF SOCIAL RELATIONSHIPS: (exhibiting nurturing behaviors; playing with dolls; interest in babies; showing empathy; interest in the welfare of the group; taking the role of the other; showing cooperation; compromise; understanding the feelings of others; intimate friendships; sharing feelings with others).
28	22	SELF-CONCEPT: (viewing self as having more control over events, as being more powerful; feeling that you have the ability to make things happen, can make a difference; being more instrumental, more effective, more ambitious).

Column Number	Variable Number	Variable Name, Codes, Instructions
29	23	ACHIEVEMENT-RELATED BEHAVIOR: (setting high levels of aspiration for one's self, often overestimating one's competence).
—	—	(WRITE IN MAJOR GOAL OF CHARACTER)
30–31	24	GOAL CLASSIFICATION: (see separate goal-classes sheet)
32	25	GOAL ACHIEVED: 0 — no 1 — yes
33	26	MAJOR MEANS USED IN TRYING TO ACHIEVE GOAL (explain in "notes") 0 — None, indefinable, uncertain. 1 — Violence (physical violence or threat with or without weapons; includes acts of war). 2 — Authority (use of legally constituted authority, legal power, calling police, lawsuits, etc.) 3 — Luck (success through fate, chance, nature, circumstance). 4 — Trickery-deceit (lying, conning others, crafty procedures). 5 — Charm (use of one's personality; charming, seducing others). 6 — Persuasion (convincing others through logic, etc.) 7 — Dependence (achieving goals through others, sponging). 8 — Personal industry (work, planning, diligence, intelligence) 9 — Other (explain) (e.g., magic, supernatural power, etc.)
34	27	MAJOR BARRIERS TO ACHIEVING GOALS (explain under "notes") 0 — No barriers, indefinable, uncertain. 1 — Violence (physical violence by others, or threat). 2 — Authority (opposition by authority, law, officials, police). 3 — Luck (defeat by fate, chance, acts of nature). 4 — Trickery-deceit (use of deceit, lying, conning by others).

Column Number	Variable Number	Variable Name, Codes, Instructions
		5 — Charm (being charmed by others).
		6 — Persuasion (being persuaded as to what course to take).
		7 — Character's own personal deficiencies (including personality problems, illness, mental blocks, stupidity, or lack of skill in coping with situations).
		8 — Personal industry of others.
		9 — Other (explain) (e.g., magic, supernatural power, etc.)
35	28	AMOUNT OF INTERACTION: (Extent to which character speaks to, works with, orders or takes orders from, all other characters in the story):
		0 — none (or very little) (e.g., store clerk)
		1 — some
		2 — much
—	—	CHARACTER SCALES: Circle the number between the two opposite adjectives which best describe personality or character of the individual as portrayed in the segment).
		PERSONALITY TRAITS:
36	29	Serious — Comic
37	30	Strong — Weak
38	31	Unselfish — Selfish
39	32	Good — Bad
40	33	Peaceful — Violent
41	34	Kind — Cruel
42	35	Intelligent — Stupid
43	36	Independent — Dependent
44	37	Warm — Cool
45	38	Honest — Dishonest
46	39	Active — Passive
		PHYSICAL CHARACTERISTICS AND APPEARANCE:
47	40	Skinny — Fat
48	41	Beautiful (Handsome) — Ugly
49	42	Agile — Clumsy
50	43	Well dressed — Sloppy

Goal Classifications

01.	Safety, self-preservation.
02.	Financial security, wealth, material success, making a living.
03.	Self-indulgence, satisfaction of impulse, comfort, leisure, escape.
04.	Thrill, adventure, pleasure.
05.	Power, mastery over others.
06.	Love, friendship, affection, companionship, sentiment.
07.	Fame, honor, prestige, recognition, popularity, reputation, respect.
08.	Justice, duty, public service, "doing what's right," preservation of law and order.
09.	Idealism for a way of life; a better world, reform, altruism.
10.	Invention, production, creation, progress, science, professional goals.
11.	Hatred, revenge, defiance, destruction, spite, fury.
12.	Self-respect, character, integrity, honesty.
13.	Respect for others, golden rule.
14.	Knowledge, education, intelligence, enlightenment.
15.	Work, industriousness, ambition.
16.	Devotion to cause or group, loyalty.
17.	Individualism, liberty, freedom, equality.
18.	Appreciation of racial, national, social, and religious differences—the brotherhood of man.
19.	Respect for our historical heritage.
20.	Appreciation of beauty, aesthetic values.
21.	Home, marriage, the family, parental duties.
22.	Morality, chastity, fidelity.
23.	Patriotism, devotion to country, military duty, etc.
24.	Religion, faith, hope, goodness, ethical values.
25.	Health, cleanliness, physical integrity.
26, 27.	(Other goals and values): please write in explanation if "other" categories are used.

CHARACTER CODE SHEET

SEGMENT: _____

CHARACTER: _____

ROLE: _____

	Seg. No. (1-3)		Ch# (4)	Sex (5)	Age (6)	Rce (7)	S.C. (8)	Ethn. (9-10)	MS (11)	Cit. (12)	Emp. (13)
OCCUPATION:											

| Occup. (14-15) | Goal (30-31) | Inc? (16) | Ach? (32) | Sty Rle (17-18) | D.R. (19) | Mns (33) | Brs (34) | Fam. Rle (20-21) | Int. (35) | Ag (22) | Act (23) | Cur (24) | Imp (25) | Anx (26) | S.R. (27) | SC (28) | Ach (29) |

MAJOR GOAL: _____

Maj

(36) serious   1 2 3 4 5 comic
(37) strong   1 2 3 4 5 weak
(38) unselfish 1 2 3 4 5 selfish
(39) good   1 2 3 4 5 bad
(40) peaceful   1 2 3 4 5 violent
(41) kind   1 2 3 4 5 cruel
(42) intelligent 1 2 3 4 5 stupid
(43) independent 1 2 3 4 5 dependent
(44) warm   1 2 3 4 5 cool

(45) honest   1 2 3 4 5 dishonest
(46) active   1 2 3 4 5 passive
(47) skinny   1 2 3 4 5 fat
(48) beautiful   1 2 3 4 5 ugly
(49) agile   1 2 3 4 5 clumsy
(50) well dressed 1 2 3 4 5 sloppy

164

NOTES:

FAMILY RELATIONSHIP SHEET

Tape # _____
Start # _____

Program Segment Title: _____

(ID NUMBER)	(SEGMENT NO.)	(FAM STRUC)	(REL)	(NATR)	(FMT)
01	02	03	04	05	06

07. Describe situations or topics dealing with family (see examples):

_____

_____

08. Describe situations or topics dealing with child training or self-development:

_____

_____

09. Describe any major family conflicts:

_____

_____

10. How was conflict resolved?

_____

_____

11. Who in the family provided or contributed most to solution of the conflict?

_____

_____

12. Describe any other problems faced by family or family members:

_____

_____

14. Who in the family provided or contributed to solution of problem?

_____

15. Who is dominant member in the family relationship?

_____

16. Describe how the *father* is portrayed in his role as parent:

_____

F ACT.	TorN?	NURTG?	STERN?	DOM?	COMPTNT?
17	18	19	20	21	22

23. Describe how the *mother* is portrayed in her role as parent.

_____

M ACT.	TorN?	NURTG?	STERN?	DOM?	COMPTNT?
24	25	26	27	28	29

30. Other comments relating to family portrayals:

_____

31. NOTES (KEY TO ABOVE):

_____

Appendix B List of Programs Monitored

Time On	Program or Program Segment Title	Length (in minutes)
WBZ-TV, Channel 4 (NBC)		
(Saturday, January 10, 1981)		
6:30 a.m.	"Carrascolendas"	28
7:00 a.m.	"¿Qué Pasa USA?"	29
7:30 a.m.	"For Kids Only"	—
7:32	"Runaways Segment"	16
7:48	"Dear Barbara"	1
7:49	"Boxing Segment"	9
8:00 a.m.	"The Godzilla/Hong Kong Phooey Hour"	—
8:00	"Hong Kong Phooey" (The Gumdrop Kid)	12
8:16	"The Beast of Storm Island"	22
8:28	"Time Out" (Running with Jim Fixx)	1
8:45	"Hong Kong Phooey" (Professor Presto)	11
8:58 a.m.	"Ask NBC News"	1
9:00 a.m.	"The Flintstones Comedy Show"	—
9:01	"Dino and Cavemouse in: Piece O'Cake"	4
9:05	"The Caveman Shuffle"	3
9:09	"Bedrock Cops in: Bedlam on the Bedrock Express"	8
9:17	"Pebbles Spelling Message"	1

Time On	Program or Program Segment Title	Length (in minutes)
9:19	"Capt. Caveman in: The Animal Master"	12
9:28	"Time Out" (Basic Skills with Gary Coleman)	1
9:36	"How to Make a Space Rocket"	2
9:37	"Education Clues"	2
9:39	"A Rocks Pox On You"	11
9:51	"How to Draw Legs"	2
9:52	"Pebbles, Dino and Bamm Bamm in: In Tune with Terror"	8
9:57	"Ask NBC News" (Inflation)	1
10:04	"Animals Dance to Classical Music"	1
10:05	"Dino and Cavemouse in: Aloha Mouse"	4
10:13	"The Gourmet Dinner"	11
10:28 a.m.	"Time Out" (Taking Lessons)	1
10:30 a.m.	"The Daffy Duck Show"	—
10:30	"A-Haunting We Will Go"	6
10:38	"Last Hungry Cat"	6
10:44	"Go Away Stowaway"	4
10:50	"Muchos Locos"	6
10:58 a.m.	"Ask NBC News" (Inflation)	1
11:00 a.m.	"Batman and the Super Seven"	—
11:01	"Batman"	17
11:20	"Super Stretch and Microwoman"	10
11:28	"Time Out" (Good nutrition)	1
11:34	"The Moon Monster"	20
11:58 a.m.	"Ask NBC News" (Endangered Wildlife)	1
12:00 p.m.	"The Johnny Quest Adventure Show"	—
12:00	"The Sea Haunt"	22
12:28 p.m.	"Time Out" (Special Olympics)	1
12:30 p.m.	"Drawing Power"	23
1:00 p.m.	"Get Off Your Block"	—
1:02	"The Gossamer Albatross" (Flying Machine)	10
1:12	"The Essex Institute in Salem"	9
1:22	"Going Straight" (About Braces)	6
(Sunday, January 18, 1981)		
7:30 a.m.	"Cool McCool"	—
7:30	"The Flying Demon"	6

Time On	Program or Program Segment Title	Length (in minutes)
7:38	"The Phantom of the Opera"	6
7:45	"The New Car"	6
7:53	"Time Out"	6
8:00 a.m.	"Mr. Magoo Show"	—
8:03	"Dr. Frankenstein"	21
8:30	"Captain Kid"	22

WNAC-TV, Channel 7 (CBS)
(Saturday, January 10, 1981)

Time On	Program or Program Segment Title	Length (in minutes)
8:00 a.m.	"The New Adventures of Mighty Mouse"	—
8:01	"Mouse of the Desert"	8
8:09	"Spinx!" (Heckle and Jeckle)	7
8:18	"Loco Motivations"	7
8:28 a.m.	"In The News" (Annual Bird Census)	2
8:30 a.m.	"The Tom and Jerry Comedy Show"	—
8:31	"Snowbrawl"	8
8:40	"Disco Droopy"	7
8:49	"Cat In The Fiddle"	7
8:56 a.m.	"In The News"	—
8:57	"The Flea Market Phenomenon"	2
9:00 a.m.	"The Bugs Bunny Road Runner Show"	—
9:03	"Hare Trimmed"	8
9:11	"Sylvester and Dogs Segment"	1
9:12	"Cheese Chasers"	7
9:19	"Zip 'n Snort"	6
9:26 a.m.	"In The News" (Not Enough Snow In West)	2
9:30 a.m.	"Bugs Bunny Road Runner Show"	—
9:31	"Fowl Weather"	7
9:37	"Rabbit of Seville"	6
9:45	"Daffy Duck and Alligators Segment"	5
9:53	"Bonanza Bunny"	6
10:00	"In The News" (The Divided Congress)	2
10:04	"Out and Out Rout"	6
10:10	"Daffy and Sheepdog Segment"	1
10:11	"Cats a-Weigh"	6
10:19	"Wind-Blown Hare"	6
10:30 a.m.	"The All New Popeye Hour"	—
10:32	"Popeye's Self Defense"	7

Time On	Program or Program Segment Title	Length (in minutes)
10:41	"The Crunch for Lunch Bunch"	7
10:49	"The Popeye Sports Parade: Fantastic Gymnastics"	11
10:56	"In The News" (Senate Majority Leader)	2
11:06	"Foggy Doggy"	10
11:18	"Bad Day at the Bakery"	6
11:27 a.m.	"In The News" (Integration Court Fight)	2
11:30 a.m.	"Drak Pak"	—
11:31	"International Graffiti"	22
11:57	"In The News" (Reagan's Trip to Mexico)	2
12:00 p.m.	"The New Fat Albert Show"	—
12:01	"The Brown Hornet"	5
12:06	"Little Brothers and Sisters Segment"	17
12:27 p.m.	"In The News" (Hostage Talks)	2
12:30 p.m.	"The Tarzan, Lone Ranger Adventure Hour"	—
12:33	"The Great Land Rush"	21
12:57	"In The News" (People Who Think Up Ideas For Toys)	2
1:00	"Tarzan, Lord of The Jungle"	22
1:27 p.m.	"In The News" (Poland)	2
1:30 p.m.	"30 Minutes"	—
1:32	"White Shadow Segment"	10
1:43	"Abused Teenagers Segment"	10
1:54	"Letters From Viewers"	2
(Tuesday, January 13, 1981)		
8:00 a.m.	"Captain Kangaroo"	50
WCVB-TV, Channel 5 (ABC)		
(Saturday, January 10, 1981)		
6:30 a.m.	"Jabberwocky" (Problem Solving)	22
7:00 a.m.	"So The Story Goes"	23
7:30 a.m.	"Barbapapa"	—
7:31	"Sheep Shearing"	3
7:35	"Barba-Bo Gets Sheared"	6
7:43	"Pottery"	5
7:51	"The Barbapapa Comb"	5
8:00 a.m.	"The Super Friends"	—

Time On	Program or Program Segment Title	Length (in minutes)
8:02	"The Invasion of the Brain Creatures"	21
8:27	"Schoolhouse Rock" (Multiplication of 6)	3
8:33	"Batman and Wonder Woman in: The Fifty-Foot Woman"	7
8:40	"Attack of the Killer Bees"	6
8:49	"The Man Beasts of Xra"	7
8:57	"Dr. Henry's Emergency Lessons for People"	1
9:00 a.m.	"The Fonz"	—
9:03	"The Vampire Strikes Back"	23
9:30 a.m.	"The Scooby Doo—Richie Rich Show"	—
9:33	"Scooby in Wonderland"	7
9:40	"Riches"	7
9:49	"Scooby's Fun Zone"	7
9:56	"Treasure Chest"	3
10:02	"Scooby's Fantastic Island"	7
10:11	"Zillion Dollar Adventures"	11
10:23	"Dr. Henry's Emergency Lessons for People"	1
10:26 a.m.	"Schoolhouse Rock" (About Planets)	3
10:30 a.m.	"Thundarr The Barbarian"	—
10:33	"Valley of the Man Apes"	20
10:54	"Doughnuts" (Assertiveness and Spending Money)	1
10:55	"Schoolhouse Rock" (Nouns)	3
11:00 a.m.	"The Heathcliff and Dingbat Show"	—
11:01	"Pumping Irony"	7
11:09	"Nutty Knights"	6
11:17	"The Watch Cat"	6
11:23	"LeManster Rally"	4
11:30 a.m.	"The Plasticman, Baby Plas Super Comedy Show"	—
11:32	"Dr. Strangeleaf"	6
11:38	"Tropical Trouble"	3
11:43	"The Hippotist"	11
11:55 a.m.	"Dear Alex and Annie"	3
(Sunday, January 18, 1981)		
7:00 a.m.	"Davey and Goliath"	—
7:01	"Editor In Chief"	14

Time On	Program or Program Segment Title	Length (in minutes)
7:15	"Man of the House"	14
7:30 a.m.	"Animals, Animals, Animals" (About Giraffes)	20
7:55	"Schoolhouse Rock" (U.S. Constitution)	3
8:00 a.m.	"Captain Bob"	—
8:08	"Drawing From Nature— Man and Beast"	24
8:30 a.m.	"Kids Are People Too"	26
8:51	"Doughnuts" (Spending and Advertising)	1

WXNE-TV, Channel 25 (Independent Station)

(Tuesday, January 13, 1981)

6:30 a.m.	"Gigglesnort Hotel"	—
6:30	"Being Yourself"	24
7:00 a.m.	"Starblazers"	20
7:30 a.m.	"Force Five"	—
7:34	"Starfire Part II"	22
8:00 a.m.	"Josie and The Pussycats"	—
8:04	"The Great Pussycat Chase"	20
8:30 a.m.	"Underdog"	—
8:31	"Fearo Part 3"	5
8:38	"Hot Air Heroes"	9
8:50	"The World of Commander McBragg"	2
8:55	"Fearo Part 4"	5
9:00 a.m.	"Lassie"	22
9:30 a.m.	"Leave It To Beaver"	23
2:00 p.m.	"Spiderwoman"	—
2:03	"The Amazon Adventure"	21
2:30 p.m.	"Kroft Superstars"	—
2:32	"Sigmund and The Sea Monsters"	23
3:00 p.m.	"Force Five"	—
3:01	"Star Fire Part II"	22
3:30 p.m.	"Starblazers"	20

(Saturday, January 17, 1981)

7:00 a.m.	"Thunderbirds"	22
7:30 a.m.	"Josie and The Pussycats"	—
7:31	"Josie and The Pussycats in Outer Space"	20
8:30 a.m.	"The Adventures of Superman"	—
8:33	"Semi-Private Eye"	22

Time On	Program or Program Segment Title	Length (in minutes)
WSBK-TV, Channel 38 (Independent)		
(Sunday, January 11, 1981)		
7:00 a.m.	"Wheelie"	—
7:03	"Wheelie and the Chopper Bunch Segment #1"	7
7:11	"Wheelie and the Chopper Bunch Segment #2"	7
7:19	"Wheelie and the Chopper Bunch Segment #3"	7
7:30 a.m.	"Valley of The Dinosaurs"	22
8:00 a.m.	"Bugs Bunny—Porky Pig"	—
8:02	"Daffy Doo"	6
8:10	"Birth of a Notion"	7
8:20	"Case of the Missing Hare"	8
8:30 a.m.	"Johnny Quest"	—
8:32	"Skull and Double Crossbones"	24
9:00 a.m.	"Popeye The Sailor"	—
9:00	"Duel to the Finish"	6
9:08	"Rain Breaker"	6
9:15	"The Spinach Scholar"	6
9:24	"Psychiatricks"	5
9:30 a.m.	"Top Cat"	25
10:00 a.m.	"The Jetsons"	25
(Tuesday, January 13, 1981)		
6:30 a.m.	"Romper Room"	25
7:00 a.m.	"Batman"	—
7:04	"The Foggiest Notion"	25
7:30 a.m.	"The New Scooby Doo Movies"	—
7:33	"Scooby Doo and The Spooky Fog"	21
8:00 a.m.	"Willie Whistle"	—
8:01	"Scaredy Cat"	7
8:11	"The Case of The Stuttering Pig"	6
8:20	"People Are Funny"	6
8:31	"Holiday For Shoestrings"	7
8:41	"Goldimouse and The 3 Cats"	6
8:50	"The Stupid Cupid"	6
(Saturday, January 17, 1981)		
8:30 a.m.	"Villa Allegre"	29
9:00 a.m.	"Carrascolendas"	—
9:01	"Don't Get In My Hair Program #2"	28
9:30 a.m.	"Hot Fudge" (Topic: Excuses)	24

Time On	Program or Program Segment Title	Length (in minutes)
WLVI-TV, Channel 56 (Independent)		
(Sunday, January 11, 1981)		
7:30 a.m.	"Big Blue Marble"	—
7:32	"Sailor Circus"	10
7:41	"Segment on Pen Pals by Bluie"	2
7:43	"Occupations: Senior Ordinary Seaman"	11
7:55 a.m.	"The Most Important Person"	—
7:56	"Segment About Eyes"	4
8:00 a.m.	"Way To Go"	22
8:29 a.m.	"Snipets"	—
8:29	"Pride"	1
8:30 a.m.	"Tom And Jerry"	—
8:30	"Father and Son Bulldogs Segment"	7
8:39	"Tom, Jerry and Woodpecker Segment"	7
8:48	"Droopy and Drippy Segment"	7
8:56	"Tom, Jerry and Bulldog Segment"	3
9:00 a.m.	"Bugs Bunny"	—
9:00	"The Hare and Turtle Race"	7
9:08	"The Lion And The Mouse Segment"	4
9:14	"Bugs Bunny Super Rabbit"	7
9:23	"The Cat Watchman"	6
9:30 a.m.	"Popeye"	—
9:30	"The Samba Dance Segment"	5
9:35	"Popeye's Testimonial Dinner"	8
9:46	"Popeye's Anthropological Expedition"	5
9:54	"The Boxing Match"	6
10:00 a.m.	"The Woody Woodpecker Show"	—
10:00	"The Case of the Gullable Woodpecker"	5
10:07	"The Cat Show"	7
10:15	"The Pied Piper"	6
10:23	"Panda Bears Cartoon"	6
10:30 a.m.	"The Flintstones"	23
11:00 a.m.	"Gilligan's Island"	23
11:30 a.m.	"The Brady Bunch"	23
(Tuesday, January 13, 1981)		
1:00 p.m.	"The Partridge Family"	22
1:30 p.m.	"The Banana Splits and Friends Show"	—

Time On	Program or Program Segment Title	Length (in minutes)
1:31	"The Adventures of Gulliver in: The Valley of Time"	21
1:56 p.m.	"The Most Important Person"	—
1:57	"Segment About Eyes"	3
2:00 p.m.	"Yogi Bear"	—
2:00	"The Baby"	5
2:08	"The Hunter"	5
2:14	"Pixie and Dixie Cartoon"	7
2:23	"Yogi Bear Cartoon"	7
2:30 p.m.	"Casper"	—
2:31	"Mother Goose Land"	8
2:40	"Mice of the Round Table"	5
2:47	"Baby Huey Cartoon"	6
2:55	"Brownie, The Juggling Bear"	5
3:00 p.m.	"Bugs Bunny"	—
3:00	"The Hare and Turtle Race"	7
3:09	"Nit Wit News"	5
3:15	"Willie The Weasel"	6
3:23	"Bugs Bunny Cartoon"	7
3:30 p.m.	"The Woody Woodpecker Show"	—
3:30	"Dualing Pianos"	7
3:40	"The Emperor Penguin"	5
3:47	"A Sleepless Night"	5
3:54	"Peace and Quiet"	6
4:00 p.m.	"The Tom And Jerry Show"	—
4:00	"Ice Follies"	6
4:08	"The Bullfight"	6
4:16	"Flying South For The Winter"	6
4:24	"The Truce"	5
4:30 p.m.	"The Flintstones"	23
(Friday, January 16, 1981)		
7:00 a.m.	"Popeye"	—
7:00	"Popeye and The Bean Stalk"	7
7:09	"Romeo"	6
7:16	"Olive Oyl For President"	5
7:24	"The 4th of July"	6
7:30 a.m.	"The Flintstones"	24
8:00 a.m.	"The Great Space Coaster"	23
8:29 a.m.	"Snipets" (About Smiles)	1
8:30 a.m.	"Fred Flintstone And Friends"	—
8:31	"Variety Segment"	6
8:38	"Goober and the Ghost Chasers"	7

Time On	Program or Program Segment Title	Length (in minutes)
8:48	"Partridge Family Adventures"	7
9:00 a.m.	"The New Zoo Revue"	22
9:11	"Snipets" (About Martin Luther King)	1
9:20	"Snipets" (About Thomas Edison)	1
9:30 a.m.	"Bozo's Big Top"	23

Appendix C Brief Descriptions
of Family and Kinship-Unit Portrayals

The following descriptions are arranged by family type (e.g., nuclear family, single parent), with the title of the program and the program-segment title (if any), and an indication as to whether the family-kinship-unit appearance was central, incidental, or irrelevant to the segment.

NUCLEAR FAMILIES

CARRASCOLENDAS (incidental)

One scene contained a Spanish family in which the father, a blacksmith, comes home from a hard day's work, and hugs and kisses his wife and children who are happy to see him.

FOR KIDS ONLY, "Dear Barbara" segment (central)

Young boy writes a letter telling of how his parents quarreled before and after their divorce and how he thinks "marriage stinks" and will stay "single forever." Barbara tells him to learn from the experience and not to give up on marriage.

THE FLINTSTONES COMEDY SHOW, "A Rocks-Pox on You" (central)

Fred, Wilma, and Pebbles are quarantined in Frank Frankenstone's house because he has a contagious disease. This prevents Fred from leaving the house to go to a hockey game. Wilma tries to be a peacemaker between Fred and Frank, who argue and fight over TV. Frank, his wife, and children are the second family unit in this episode.

THE FLINTSTONES COMEDY SHOW, "The Gourmet Dinner" (central)

Hilda Frankenstone has to go away with her children to be with her husband, who is away on his birthday. She asks the Flintstones to take care of the house in her absence.

BARBAPAPA, "Barba Bo Gets Sheared" (central)

Little Barba Bo wants to help the family with sheep shearing and accidentally gets sheared himself. Bo's brother solves the problems by weaving a coat from his sheared wool until Bo's can grow back.

BARBAPAPA (segment on pottery and sculpture) (incidental)

Barba Bo tries to teach his brother (Barba Bright) how to do pottery, but he fails to do it well and is unhappy. His sisters help save the day by turning themselves into clay vases to make him happy.

THE SUPERFRIENDS SHOW, "Attack of the Killer Bees" (irrelevant)

Families in an African village are working in the fields when attacked by killer bees. Superfriends Aquaman and Samurai trap the bees and save the villagers.

THE SCOOBY DOO-RICHIE RICH SHOW, "Treasure Chest" (central)

Mr. Rich and wife are awakened by noise from a device which invents things. He calls his son Richie, who attempts to solve the noise problem in the garage. Mr. Rich eventually destroys the machine.

THE PLASTICMAN, BABY PLAS SUPER COMEDY SHOW, "Dr. Strangeleaf" (incidental)

Plasticman, wife Penny, and Baby Plas are involved. Penny enters and wins a flower show. Dr. Strangeleaf creates plant monsters to eat up all plants in the city, so he can win the contest himself. He is stopped by Plasticman and Baby Plas.

DEAR ALEX AND ANNIE (central)

A 14-year-old girl has written a letter in which she says she is embarrassed for her mother, who is pregnant again, because she thinks her mother is "too old." Alex and Annie tell her she is embarrassed for herself, that parents are people in love, and that she will get over her embarrassment and will be the envy of her friends when the baby comes.

DAVEY AND GOLIATH, "Man of the House" (central)

Davey's parents must go out of town for the day and leave Davey in charge of the house and his sister. Davey and friends play and he neglects his responsibilities. Father then explains the interrelationship of responsibility, fun, and freedom.

KIDS ARE PEOPLE TOO (Wendy Holcombe segment) (central)
Wendy tells of how her father would not let her play his banjo, but she helped her mother, who then let her play it. Father was angry at first but relented when he found out she could play it—and he gave it to her.

KIDS ARE PEOPLE TOO ("Runaways" segment) (central)
Female child who ran away from home tells of father who beat her for going out without telling him, and of parental pressure to do well in school.

NEW FAT ALBERT SHOW, "Little Brothers and Sisters" (central)
Dum Donald finds out he's going to get a little brother or sister and is upset and jealous. After little sister arrives, Donald likes her but doesn't want his friends to know. Donald's father tells Donald where babies come from and that since he has been such a good child, they decided to have another.

THE TARZAN-LONE RANGER ADVENTURE HOUR, "The Great Land Rush" (central)
A family of Irish immigrants competes with criminals for a choice piece of land, with the Lone Ranger and Tonto coming to the rescue. During the story, the young daughter falls from a wagon and is lost. After much parental concern, she is found and returned by the Lone Ranger.

30 MINUTES, "Abused Teenagers" (central)
Interview with a teenager who started a self-help program and with the father, who had beaten his children until he received help through Parents Anonymous, and who now is supporting his daughter's teen group.

LEAVE IT TO BEAVER (central)
Wally is yelled at for coming in late and missing dinner. The next day Mrs. Cleaver finds a letter from the merchant marine and the Cleavers suspect Wally is planning to run away from home. Actually it is Lumpy, Wally's friend, who is planning to run away, and his father doesn't know it. Lumpy talks with Mr. Cleaver and decides not to run away.

KROFT SUPER STARS, "Sigmund and the Sea Monsters" (incidental)
Sweet Mama leaves pet lobster Prince at the cave while she goes to

the hairdresser. When his father doesn't watch him, Prince runs away to Sigmund, who sends him back to cave.

STARBLAZERS (incidental)

Derek and Conroy capture a Gamelon pilot on a scouting mission. Major plot deals with earth being destroyed by Gamelon bombs. Subplot involves jealousy between Derek and brother Alex, who returns home from the Space Academy.

VALLEY OF THE DINOSAURS (central)

The Butler family and others are picking berries and are chased away by Scalac. Pet dinosaur Glump falls in a hole and is surrounded by wolves. Family cooperates to rescue Glump and chase dinosaurs away in the Valley of Smoking Water. This also includes the cave family, which cooperates in the rescue and in fighting dinosaurs.

JETSONS (central)

George and Jane are going on a second honeymoon to Las Venus. There, his boss calls and demands George close a deal with G.G. Galaxy, a woman head of another company. As he is entertaining G.G., he is afraid his wife will think he is "fooling around." Jane finds them together, but all is O.K. when G.G. explains the situation to Jane.

WILLIE WHISTLE, "Goldimouse and the Three Cats" (cartoon) (central)

Begins as a take-off on Goldilocks story. When three cats return home, the spoiled one wants to eat a mouse instead of his porridge. Father Sylvester calls him a spoiled brat, dumps porridge on his head, and says he will catch a mouse.

BIG BLUE MARBLE (occupations segment) (incidental)

Tony, a 17-year-old English seaman, shows his parents around the Queen Elizabeth II.

THE FLINTSTONES, "Mom's House" (central)

Upon learning that Wilma's mother might come to live with them, Fred buys a cheap old house for her to live in. When Fred and Barney spend much time to fix it, their wives think they are cheating on them. The house is flooded and destroyed, but mother-in-law is not coming after all.

YOGI BEAR (no segment title) (central)

Yogi tries to steal a sandwich from a picnicking family but gets caught. The baby gets out of its pen and when Yogi rescues her from animals, mother thinks he is bothering the baby and calls the ranger.

THE FLINTSTONES (camping segment) (central)

Fred and Barney go camping and leave Wilma and Betty at home. After cleaning house and caring for the children, the wives go camping to prove to the husbands they are good campers. With the aid of a new neighbor, Samantha (from "Bewitched"), they scare husbands, who apologize. Finally, the girls don't like to swim in cold water so they say they are out of milk and go home.

THE FLINTSTONES, "The Way Outs" (incidental)

Fred's club is having its annual costume party. Fred dresses like spaceman and is mistaken for a Way Out—a member of a new musical group coming to Bedrock to entertain. Eventually all is well and Fred wins best-costume prize.

EXTENDED FAMILY

¿QUÉ PASA, USA? (central)

This involves several levels of extended-family relationships, with a mother, father, son and daughter, and two grandparents in the household. Story revolves around a female cousin who has married a Jewish-American, and much of the plot involves family disputes about this mixed marriage of the Cuban-Catholic cousin and her Jewish spouse. There is a gradual acceptance of the marriage, however, which is affirmed when it is announced that the cousin is pregnant.

THE BRADY BUNCH, "The Wedding" (central)

This deals with the marriage of two widowed adults, both of whom have growing children who display jealousy toward their stepbrothers and stepsisters. After a chaotic wedding reception, the parents go on a honeymoon, feel guilty about their children, and finally invite them on the honeymoon.

SINGLE PARENT—FEMALE

FOR KIDS ONLY (segment on runaways) (central)

Interview with black female teen who couldn't get along with her mother and ran away. After staying at Place Runaway House, she and her mother now are making efforts to get along better.

DRAWING POWER, "Turkey of the Week" (incidental)

One short segment of several in the program in which a boy, Dirty Harry, is a mess and doesn't care. Mother has no control over him. He finally learns a hygiene lesson when even his dog leaves him because he is such a mess.

DAVEY AND GOLIATH, "Editor-in-Chief" (incidental)

Davey is delivery boy for a newspaper, whose editor gives him a small printing press. Davey works hard to thank editor. Mother explains to Davey that he should think of a way on his own to thank the editor—which he does.

SCHOOLHOUSE ROCK (segment on the U.S. Constitution) (incidental)

Brief portrayal of a mother in a voting line with daughter, whom she drags away after voting.

CAPTAIN KANGAROO, "Simon in the Land of Chalk Drawings" (central)

A segment of a larger program that deals with a child who sulks when scolded by his mother. After his mother tells him to look at himself sulking, he looks in a mirror and draws himself sulking. When he visits the Land of Chalk Drawings, he finds that his sulking self has changed the drawings. Then he draws a smile on his sulking self and promises to always smile.

THE PARTRIDGE FAMILY, "The Whale" (central)

Mother disciplines son, and helps family solve problem of recording a "whale-music" album.

CASPER (no segment title) (irrelevant)

Casper in Mother Goose Land frolics with Little Red Riding Hood and frightens the old woman who lives in a shoe, who then gathers her children and hops away (in her shoe).

CASPER (Baby Huey) (incidental)

Mother leaves Baby Huey on Christmas Eve to go shopping. In her absence, a hungry fox tries to eat Huey, who blows the fox out of his fur with a bomb present. Upon her return, Huey gives mother fur as an Xmas present.

BUGS BUNNY (no segment title) (incidental)

Mother hen leaves her chicks at home to get the doctor for her sick chick son Wilbur. Meanwhile, Willie the Weasel, posing as a doctor, tries to eat the chicks, but is beaten off. Real doctor comes with mother and gives Wilbur castor oil.

POPEYE (no segment title) (central)

In a version of Jack and the Beanstalk, Popeye's mother tells him how poor they are. He trades his car for a can of spinach, which eventually sprouts large stalk that Popeye climbs; he beats up the giant and saves the hen that lays golden eggs.

FRED FLINTSTONE AND FRIENDS, "Partridge Family Adventures" (central)

Cousin comes to sing with Partridge family. He is not a good singer but mother and family don't want to tell him.

SINGLE PARENT—MALE

THE WOODY WOODPECKER SHOW (Panda bears cartoon) (incidental)

When Woody pesters pandas by pecking on their house, father panda tries to catch him. The lazy and inept father cannot catch the woodpecker, whereas son does by putting salt on his tail.

THUNDERBIRDS (no segment title) (incidental)

Story about a spy trying to steal secret photos of Alpha 2-0. The two sons of Col. Carl Jamison are trapped in a mine shaft and are rescued by the Tracy family—a father and three sons who head International Rescue.

TOM AND JERRY (cartoon—no title) (central)

Conflict is created with father and son bulldogs when Tom is chasing Jerry. Father is extremely protective of his young son and beats up Tom repeatedly.

THE BUGS BUNNY ROAD RUNNER HOUR (cartoon—no title) (central)

Butch, a father bulldog, forces the cat to let his son chew on his tail, by beating him up. Father is aggressive and protective of his son.

SO THE STORY GOES, "The Willow Story" (central)

One of several stories in the larger program of legends, this segment deals with a father who is possessive of his daughter. After he has arranged a marriage for her and kept her a prisoner, she escapes with her true love.

THE FLINTSTONES COMEDY SHOW, "Bedlam on the Bedrock Express" (irrelevant)

In a story about a gold robbery, a little girl's bike is taken and she gets her father to go after those who stole it.

THE HEATHCLIFF AND DINGBAT SHOW, "Nutty Knights" (incidental)

Trapped in another time period, Dingbat and the Creeps rescue the king's daughter, Fair Maiden, who has been kidnapped by Sir Grimacelot.

BARBAPAPA (sheep-shearing segment) (central)

This segment involves the father, daughter, and son and is about shearing sheep in the summer and the use of wool in the winter. When the son has a new idea for more efficient shearing, he is encouraged by his father to try it.

THE SCOOBY DOO-RICHIE RICH SHOW, "Scooby's Fantastic Island" (irrelevant)

Caught in a prehistoric time period, the heroes are involved in a struggle with a caveman, who, at one point, offers his daughter to one of the heroes for a favor done.

THE FLINTSTONE FAMILY SHOW, "Pebbles's Spelling Message" (incidental)

In a brief segment, Pebbles is given a scrambled word and helps Fred to spell out the word "father."

THE PLASTICMAN, BABY PLAS SUPER COMEDY SHOW "Tropical Trouble" (incidental)

Plasticman allows Baby Plas to play outside on a tropical island; Baby is caught by a Gorilla who mothers him.

LEAVE IT TO BEAVER (no subtitle) (central)

This segment involves a father, Mr. Rutherford, and his teenage son Lumpy, who plans to run away from home because his father had taken the car keys away from him. Situation is resolved when the Cleaver family becomes involved.

THE WOODY WOODPECKER SHOW, "The Cat Show" (incidental)

Cartoon about father and son pandas who try to bathe a cat. The selfish and clumsy father yells at his son.

BUGS BUNNY, "Nit Wit News" (incidental)

In a theater, a child duck gets away from his father into the projection booth and gets caught in the projector.

BUGS BUNNY-ROAD RUNNER SHOW, "Cats-A-Weigh" (incidental)

Sylvester the Cat and son get jobs on a ship as mousers. Father makes son chase the little mice but is beaten up when he mistakes a kangaroo for a large mouse.

BATMAN AND THE SUPER SEVEN (no subtitle) (irrelevant)

In the story, Barbara Gordon tells her father that Batgirl is not responsible for a theft. This is a minor incident in the adventure.

BATMAN (no subtitle) (irrelevant)

Only minor contact occurs between Commissioner Gordon and daughter Barbara (Batgirl) when he calls her on the police radio to warn her.

BATMAN, "The Foggiest Notion" (irrelevant)

Two father-daughter pairs are identified but interact little in this episode.

JOHNNY QUEST, "Skull and Double Crossbones" (incidental)

Dr. Quest helps guide and advise son Johnny in this treasure-island type of adventure.

THE JOHNNY QUEST ADVENTURE SHOW, "The Sea Hunt" (incidental)

Dr. Quest and son Johnny again participate in an ocean adventure with a Dutch ship and a sea monster.

FORCE FIVE, "Star Fire—Part II" (incidental)

The father, Dr. Copernicus, is involved in saving his son's life in this story about the invasion and destruction of the earth by the Pandemonium Empire.

FOR KIDS ONLY (runaway-children segment) (central)

Story told by a teenage runaway son who didn't get along with his father. The son also used drugs. With the help of Place Runaway House, father and son are working toward a better relationship.

MARRIED COUPLES

BUGS BUNNY SHOW (no subtitle) (central)

A married alligator's unhatched egg is threatened when Daffy Duck mistakes it for his and Mrs. Duck's. Daffy resists sitting on egg and fights with his wife. Male alligator saves his own egg.

DOUGHNUTS (no segment title) (central)

A short segment about assertiveness and spending money. This deals with a meek and mild Henry Dimble, who bought a present for his wife's birthday that she didn't need. He is sent back to the store for something more reasonable, and learns not to be so meek.

GILLIGAN'S ISLAND (no subtitle) (incidental)

The Howells work together to use a robot to escape from the island.

THE FLINTSTONES (no subtitle) (incidental)

In an episode including three family groups, Samantha and Darren Stevens represent the married couple. This segment involves Darren's going camping for the weekend and not wanting his wife to go because "it's not the sort of thing for a woman."

THE FLINTSTONES COMEDY SHOW, "Aloha Mouse" (irrelevant)

Fred and Wilma are a married couple on a vacation. A brief plot revolves around a cavemouse and Dino in chase scenes around the ship.

¿QUÉ PASA, USA? (no subtitle) (central)

Patricia and Gary are a newly married couple with different religions. They are confronted by opposition from members of their extended family who are having difficulty accepting their mixed marriage.

THE FLINTSTONE FAMILY ADVENTURES, "The Gourmet Dinner" (incidental)

Fred invites his boss and spouse, Mr. and Mrs. Slate, to a gourmet dinner. When Mrs. Slate faints after finding out what is in her soup, Mr. Slate gives Fred a raise.

PLASTICMAN AND BABY PLAS COMEDY SHOW, "The Hippotist" (incidental)

Plasticman and wife, Penny, work together to catch the Hippotist who hypnotizes bankers to get all their jewels. They fail.

IN THE NEWS (new Senate Majority Leader Howard Baker) (irrelevant)

One reference here was to Senator Baker's relatives and wife, whose father was formerly Senate minority leader.

WILLIE WHISTLE, "The Stupid Cupid" (cartoon) (central)

Daffy, a married duck, gets into trouble with a rooster when he is shot by cupid's arrow and tries to make out with a chicken.

SIBLINGS ONLY

BARBAPAPA, "The New Hairdo" (central)

Story involves brother and sisters Barba Bo, Barba Bright, Barba Lib, and Barba Lolla, who get involved in giving Barba Bo a new hairdo.

THE SUPERFRIENDS, "The Invasion of Brain Creatures" (incidental)

The Wonder Twins, Sand and Jana, are captured and tied to a speed boat by Superman and Batman, whose minds have been tampered with.

They escape by changing themselves into, respectively, an ice jet and a big hawk.

SCHOOLHOUSE ROCK (segment on nouns) (irrelevant)
A girl and her brother in this brief segment are attacked by a dog.

THE NEW FAT ALBERT SHOW, "Little Brothers and Sisters" (central)
Two pairs of sibling are shown. One big brother, Weird Harold, ends up carrying his protesting little sister home for supper. Another big brother forces his little brother home to take a bath by pushing him down the street.

THE LONE RANGER, "The Great Land Rush" (incidental)
The brothers in this episode are criminals who are trying illegally to attain a piece of land at the expense of another family.

JOSIE AND THE PUSSYCATS, "The Great Pussycat Chase" (incidental)
Alex saves his sister Alexandra's life in this around-the-world adventure with Shadow.

JOSIE AND THE PUSSYCATS, "Josie and the Pussycats in Outer Space" (irrelevant)
Alex and Alexandra are members of the group in an adventure on the planet run by cat people.

HOT FUDGE (segment on excuses) (irrelevant)
Mona and Jeffrey are brother-and-sister puppet characters who appear separately in this short segment.

WAY TO GO, "Mystery of the Gingerbread House" (irrelevant)
A continuing drama: Here, a physically handicapped girl is searching for her grandmother and is helped by two brothers.

TOM AND JERRY SHOW (a Droopy and Drippy cartoon) (irrelevant)
These twins interact little in this segment about Droopy, a butler in a mansion. He does get his brother a job in the mansion and Drippy, the stronger, helps protect him from a stranger.

YOGI BEAR (a Pixie and Dixie cartoon) (incidental)
Pixie and Dixie try to arrange a home for a strong flea on the cat. Most of the action revolves around Jinx, the cat, and his battles with the flea.

FRED FLINTSTONE AND FRIEND, "Goober and the Ghostchasers" (incidental)

Twin brothers Dunk and Dink represent opposites in personality and are in conflict throughout the episode, which takes place on a pirate ship.

AUNTS AND NEPHEWS

THE GODZILLA/HONG KONG PHOOEY HOUR, "The Beast of Storm Island" (incidental)

Aunt Quinn and nephew Pete are part of crew of a ship that seeks refuge at Storm Island. She cares for Pete when he catches cold.

SPIDERWOMAN, "The Amazon Adventure" (incidental)

Jessica, alias Spiderwoman, is Billy's aunt and they destroy an Incan empire.

UNCLES AND NEPHEWS

THE DAFFY DUCK SHOW, "A-Haunting We Will Go" (central)

Daffy's nephew goes trick-or-treating, is scared by an old witch, and runs home. Daffy tries to prove to his nephew that he shouldn't be afraid by going back to the old house, where he is almost cooked for dinner by the witch.

THE DAFFY DUCK SHOW, "Muchos Locos" (incidental)

Speedy Gonzales tells his nephew stories about stupid cats and stupid ducks. Upon overhearing this, Daffy clobbers Speedy with a club.

THE SCOOBY DOO AND RICHIE RICH SHOW, "Scooby in Wonderland" (incidental)

Shaggy tells Scooby and nephew Scrappy a bedtime story. In a dream sequence, Scooby and the others play out the Alice in Wonderland story, which turns into a nightmare for him.

THE SCOOBY DOO AND RICHIE RICH SHOW, "Scooby's Fun Zone" (incidental)

Scooby and nephew get into various sorts of mischief and danger at a carnival.

THE SCOOBY DOO AND RICHIE RICH SHOW, "Scooby's Fantastic Island" (incidental)

Shaggy, Scooby, and Scrappy are fishing. A large fish pulls their boat through a time zone to a prehistoric island where they are chased by a caveman. Scooby is protective of his nephew Scrappy, trying to keep him out of trouble.

TOP CAT (no subtitle) (incidental)

Top Cat is in a tussle with crooked cops—an uncle (sergeant) Eugene and his nephew, officer Prowler—who try to discredit a fellow officer so that the nephew can take over his beat. Top Cat saves the day by utilizing his own dirty tricks.

POPEYE, "The Fourth of July" (central)

Episode revolves around Popeye trying to teach his mischievous nephews not to play with fireworks. He succeeds only after nephews are blown skyward on a skyrocket and are saved by Popeye.

UNCLE AND NIECE

THE ALL NEW POPEYE HOUR, "Foggy Doggy" (irrelevant)

In the first scene, uncle Dudley is shown as a rather silly, clumsy, and grouchy uncle who complains to his two nieces about the cost of feeding the dog. The remainder of the adventure involves a dumb-blonde niece who, to please the uncle, tries to get a job, mistakes an ad for a light housekeeper, ends up at a lighthouse, and is terrorized by a "fog beast."

COUSINS

GIGGLESNORT HOTEL, "Being Yourself" (irrelevant)

Maynard's cousin Sheepdog is a big TV star who tells everyone to wear the latest fashions of a polkadot bandana, a flower, and a ring in their nose. Most conform, but find that Sheepdog is simply trying to make money. They are angry and learn a lesson about being themselves.

GRANDMOTHER AND GRANDDAUGHTER

BUGS BUNNY-ROAD RUNNER SHOW, "Wind Blown Hare" (irrelevant)

Bugs Bunny is Little Red Riding Hood in a spoof on several fairy tales.

GRANDMOTHER AND GRANDSON

THE HEATHCLIFF AND DINGBAT SHOW, "The Watch Cat" (irrelevant)

The purple fink burglar tries to rob Heathcliff's house. A little grandson tries to comfort his grandmother who is worried about the burglar in the neighborhood.

Bibliography

TV AND SEX ROLES

Action for Children's Television.. *New views on TV viewing.* Pamphlet prepared and distributed by ACT, Newtonville, Mass., 1981.

Bandura, A. *Principles of behavior modification.* New York: Holt, Rinehart & Winston, 1969.

Bandura, A. *Social learning theory.* Englewood Cliffs, N.J.: Prentice-Hall, 1977.

Bandura, A., Ross, D., and Ross, S. A. Imitation of film-mediated aggressive models. *Journal of Abnormal and Social Psychology.* 1963, *66*, 3–11.

Bandura, A. and Walters, R. H. *Social learning and personality development.* New York: Holt, Rinehart & Winston, 1963.

Barcus, F. E. *Television in the after-school hours.* Newtonville, Mass.: Action for Children's Television, 1975.

Barcus, F. E. *Weekend children's television.* Newtonville: Action for Children's Television, 1975b.

Barcus, F. E. *Commercial children's television on weekends and weekday afternoons.* Newtonville: Action for Children's Television, 1978a.

Barcus, F. E. (with Wolkin, R.). *Children's television: An analysis of programming and advertising.* New York: Praeger, 1977.

Beuf, A. Doctor, lawyer, household drudge. *Journal of Communication.* 1974, *24* (2), 142–145.

Busby, L. J. Defining the sex-role standard in network children's programs. *Journalism Quarterly,* 1974 *51*, 690–696.

Busby, L. J. Sex-role research on the mass media. *Journal of Communication,* 1975, *25* (4), 107–131.

Butler, M., and Paisley, W. *Women and the mass media.* New York: Human Sciences Press, 1980.

Cantor, M. G. Women and public broadcasting. *Journal of Communication,* 1977, *27* (1), 14–19.

Cathey-Calvert, C. Sexism on "Sesame Street:" Outdated concepts in a "progressive" program. 1977. *Resources in Education* (ERIC Document Reproduction Service No. ED 168–683).

Clark, C. C. Television and social control: Some observations on the portrayal of ethnic minorities. *Television Quarterly,* 1969, *8,* 18–22.

Clark, C. Race, identification and television violence. In G. A. Comstock, E. A. Rubinstein, and J. P. Murray (eds.), *Television and social behavior.* Vol. 5, *Television's effects: Further explorations.* Washington, D.C.: Government Printing Office, 1972.

Collins, W. A. The developing child as viewer. *Journal of Communication,* 1975, *25* (4), 35–44.

Comstock, G. The effects of television on children and adolescents: The evidence so far. *Journal of Communication,* 1975, *25* (4), 25–34.

Courtney, A. E., and Whipple, T. Women in TV commercials. *Journal of Communication,* 1974, *24* (2), 110–118.

Culley, J. D., and Bennett, R. Selling women, selling blacks. *Journal of Communication,* Autumn 1976, *26* (4), 160–174.

Culley, J. D., Lazer, W., and Atkin, C. K. The experts look at children's television. *Journal of Broadcasting,* 1976, *20* (1), 3–21.

Davidson, E. S., Yasuna, A., and Tower, A. The effects of television cartoons on sex-role stereotyping in young girls. *Child Development,* 1979, *50* (2), 597–600.

DeFleur, M. L. Occupational roles as portrayed on television. *Public Opinion Quarterly,* 1964, *28,* 57–74.

DeFleur, M., and DeFleur, L. The relative contribution of television as a learning source for children's occupational knowledge. *American Sociological Review,* 1967, *32,* 777–789.

Dohrmann, R. A gender profile on children's educational TV. *Journal of Communication,* 1975, *25* (4), 56–65.

Donagher, P. C., Poulos, R. W., Liebert, R. M., and Davidson, E. S. Race, sex and social example: An analysis of character portrayals on inter-racial television entertainment. *Sociological Reports,* 1975, *37,* 1023–1034.

Downing, M. Heroine of the daytime serial. *Journal of Communication,* 1974, *24* (2), 130–137.

Editorial research reports on the changing American family. Washington, D.C.: Congressional Quarterly, 1979.

Feldman, R. S., Vorwerk, K. E., and Rood, P. Modeling processes in the development of sex-role-related performance expectation. 1977. *Resources in Education* (ERIC Document Reproduction Service No. ED 142–921).

Flake-Hobson, C., Skeen, P., and Robinsons, B. E. Review of theories and research concerning sex-role development and androgeny with suggestions for teachers. *Family Relations,* 1980, *29,* 155–162.

Forisha, B. L. *Sex roles and personal awareness.* Morristown, N.J.: General Learning Press, 1978.

Frueh, T., and McGhee, P. E. Traditional sex-role development and amount of time spent watching television. *Developmental Psychology,* 1975, *11,* 109.

Goff, D. H., Dysart, L., and Lehrer, S. K. Sex-role portrayals of selected female television characters. *Journal of Broadcasting,* 1980, *24* (4), 467–478.

Greenberg, B. S. *Life on television: Content analyses of U.S. TV drama.* Norwood, N.J.: Ablex Publishing, 1980.

Greenberg, B., and Gordon, T. R. Social class and racial differences in children's perceptions of television violence. In G. A. Comstock, E. A. Rubinstein, and J. P. Murray (eds.), *Television and social behavior,* Vol. 5, *Television's effects: Further explorations.* Washington, D.C.: Government Printing Office, 1972.

Grusec, J. E., and Brinker, D. B. Reinforcement for imitation as a social learning determinant with implications for sex-role development. *Journal of Personality and Social Psychology,* 1972, *21,* 149–158.

Hall, C. S., and Lindzey, G. *Theories of personality.* 2nd ed. New York: Wiley, 1970.

Hartley, R. E., and Hardesty, F. P. Children's perceptions of sex roles in childhood. *Journal of Genetic Psychology,* 1964, *105,* 43–51.

Hays, H. R. *The dangerous sex.* New York: Pocket Books, 1972.

Head, S. W. Content analysis of television dramatic programs. *Quarterly of Film, Radio, and Television,* 1954, *9,* 175–194.

Heinemann, G. A. Children's programming. *Journal of Broadcasting,* 1981, *25* (3), 309–310.

Himmelweit, H. T., Oppenheim, A. N., and Vince, P. *Television and the child.* New York: Oxford University Press, 1958.

Isber, C., and Cantor, M. G. *Report of the task force on women in public broadcasting.* Washington, D.C.: Corporation of Public Broadcasting, 1976.

Journal of Communication. Women: Nine reports on role, image, and message. Spring 1974, *24* (2), 103–156.

Kagan, J. Acquisition and significance of sex-typing and sex-role identity. In M. L. Hoffman and L. W. Hoffman (eds.), *Review of child development research,* Vol. 1. New York: Russell Sage Foundation, 1964.

Katz, P. A. Determinants of sex-role flexibility in children. 1979. *Resources in Education* (ERIC Document Reproduction Service No. ED 179 290).

Kilbourne, J. The changing images of females and males in television commercials: Plus ca change, plus c'est la meme chose. Ph.D. dissertation, Boston University, 1980.

Kohlberg, L. A. A cognitive-developmental analysis of children's sex-role concepts and attitudes. In E. Maccoby (ed.), *The development of sex differences.* Stanford: Stanford University Press, 1966.

Leifer, A. D., Gordon, N. J., and Graves, S. B. Children's television: More than mere entertainment. *Harvard Educational Review,* 1974, *44* (2), 213–245.

Lemon, J. Women and blacks on prime-time television. *Journal of Communication,* 1977, *26* (4), 70–78.

Levinson, R. M. From Olive Oyl to Sweet Polly Purebread: Sex role stereotypes and televised cartoons. *Journal of Popular Culture,* 1975, *9* (3), 561–572.

Liebert, R. M., Neale, J. M., and Davidson, E. S. *The early window: Effects of television on children and youth.* Elmsford, N.Y.: Pergamon, 1973.

Long, M. L., and Simon, R. J. The roles and statuses of women on children and family programs. *Journalism Quarterly,* 1974, *51,* 107–110.

Lyle, J., and Hoffman, H. Children's use of television and other media. In E. A. Rubinstein, G. A. Comstock, and J. P. Murray (eds.), *Television and social behavior,* Vol. 4, *Television in day-to-day life: Patterns of use.* Washington, D.C.: Government Printing Office, 1972a.

Lyle, J., and Hoffman, H. R. Explorations in patterns of television viewing by preschool-age children. In E. A. Rubinstein, G. A. Comstock, and J. P. Murray (eds.), *Television and social behavior,* Vol. 4, *Television in day-to-day life: Patterns of use.* Washington, D.C.: U.S. Government Printing Office, 1972b.

Maccoby, E., and Jacklin, C. N. *The psychology of sex differences.* Stanford: Stanford University Press, 1974.

Mankiewics, F., and Swerdlow, J. Sex roles in TV: Co-opted liberation. *Television Quarterly,* 1977–78, *14* (1), 5–17.

Mayes, S. L., and Valentine, K. B. Sex role stereotyping in Saturday morning cartoon shows. *Journal of Broadcasting,* 1979, *23* (1), 41–50.

McArthur, L. Z., and Eisen, S. V. Television and sex-role stereotyping. *Journal of Applied Social Psychology.* 1976, *6* (4), 329–351.

McNeil, J. C. Feminism, femininity, and the television series: A content analysis. *Journal of Broadcasting,* 1975, *19* (3), 259–271.

Mead, M. *Male and female: A study of the sexes in a changing world.* New York: Morrow, 1950.

Media Women's Association (eds.), *Rooms with no view: A woman's guide to the man's world of the media.* New York: Harper and Row, 1974.

Meyer, T. P. Children's perceptions of their favorite TV characters as behavioral models. *Educational Broadcasting Review,* 1973, *7,* 28–33.

Miller, M. M., and Reeves, B. Dramatic TV content and children's sex-role stereotypes. *Journal of Broadcasting,* 1976, *20* (1), 35–50.

Mischel, W. A social-learning view of sex difference. In E. Maccoby (ed.), *The development of sex differences.* Stanford: Stanford University Press, 1966.

Mischel, W. Sex-typing and socialization. In P. H. Mussen (ed.), *Carmichael's manual of child psychology.* New York: Wiley, 1970.

Mischel, W. Toward a cognitive social learning reconceptualization of personality. *Psychological Review,* 1974, *80,* 252–283.

Money, J. Developmental differentiation of feminity and masculinity compared. In S. Farber et al. (eds.), *Man and civilization: The potential of woman.* New York: McGraw-Hill, 1963.

Money, J. The sexes: Biological imperatives. *Time,* January 8, 1973, p. 34.

Murray, J. P. *Television and youth: 25 years of research and controversy.* Boys Town, Nb.: Boys Town Press, 1980.

Mussen, P. H. Early sex-role development. In D. A. Goslin (ed.), *Handbook of socialization theory and research.* Chicago: Rand McNally, 1969.

Mussen, P. H., Conger, J. J., and Kagan, J. *Child development and personality,* 3rd ed. New York: Harper and Row, 1969.

Nadelman, L. Sex identity in American children: Memory, knowledge, and preference tests. *Developmental Psychology,* 1974, *10,* 417–437.

Nadelson, C. M. Adjustment: New approach to women's mental health. In *The American Woman: Who Will She Be?* M. L. McBee and K. A. Blake (eds.). Beverly Hills: Glencoe Press, 1974, 21–36.

National Organization for Women. *Women in the wasteland fight back: A report on the image of women portrayed in television programming.* Pittsburgh: Know, Inc., 1972.

Nolan, J. D., Galst, J. P., and White, M. A. Sex bias on children's televison programs. *Journal of Psychology,* 1977, *96,* 197–204.

Nova. The pinks and the blues. Program originally broadcast on Public Broadcasting System (PBS) in September 1980. Copyright: WGBH Educational Foundation, 1980.

O'Kelly, C. Sexism in children's television. *Journalism Quarterly,* 1974, *51,* 722–724.

Osofsky, J. D., and Osofsky, H. H. Androgeny as a life style. *Family Coordinator,* 1972, *21,* 43–50.

Palmer, E. L., and Dorr, A. *Children and the faces of television.* New York: Academic Press, 1980.

Perloff, R. M. Some antecedents of children's sex-role stereotypes. *Psychological Reports,* 1977, *40* (2), 463–466.

Perry, D. G., and Perry, L. C. Observational learning in children: Effects of sex of model and subject's sex role behavior. *Journal of Personality and Social Psychology,* 1975, *31,* 1083–1088.

Reeves, B., and Miller, M. M. A multidimensional measure of children's identification with television characters. *Journal of Broadcasting,* 1978, *22* (1), 71–86.

Schau, C. G., and Busch, J. W. Multidimensional aspects of young children's sex-role development. 1979. *Resources in Education* (ERIC Document Reproduction Service No. ED 174–356).

Scherer, K. R. Stereotype change following exposure to counter-stereotypical media heroes. *Journal of Broadcasting,* 1970–71, *15* (1), 91–100.

Schramm, W., Lyle, J., and Parker, E. B. *Television in the lives of children.* Stanford: Stanford University Press, 1961.

Sears, R. R., Rau, L., and Alpert, R. *Identification and child rearing.* Stanford: Stanford University Press, 1965.

Seggar, J. F. Imagery of women in television drama: 1974. *Journal of Broadcasting*, 1975, *19* (3), 273–282.

Seggar, J. F., Hafen, J. K., and Hannonen-Gladden, H. Television's portrayals of minorities and women in drama and comedy drama 1971–80. *Journal of Broadcasting*, 1981, *25* (3), 277–288.

Seggar, J. F., and Wheeler, P. World of work on TV: Ethnic and sex representation in TV drama. *Journal of Broadcasting*, 1973, *17* (2), 201–214.

Shechtman, S. A. Occupational portrayal of men and women on the most frequently mentioned television shows of pre-school children. 1978. *Resource in Education* (ERIC Document Reproduction Service No. ED 174-356).

Stein, A. H., and Friedrich, L. K. (with Vondracek, F.). Television content and young children's behavior. In J. P. Murray, E. A. Rubinstein, and G. A. Comstock (eds.), *Television and social behavior*, Vol. 2, *Television and social learning*. Washington, D.C.: Government Printing Office, 1972.

Stein, A. H., Pohly, S. R., and Mueller, E. The influences of masculine, feminine, and neutral tasks on children's achievement behavior, expectancies of success, and attainment values. *Child Development*, 1971, *42*, 195–207.

Sternglanz, S. H., and Serbin, L. A. Sex-role stereotyping in children's television programs. *Developmental Psychology*, 1974, *10* (5), 710–715.

Streicher, H. W. The girls in the cartoons. *Journal of Communication*, 1974, *24* (2), 125–129.

Tavris, C., and Offir, C. *The longest war: Sex differences in perspective*. New York: Harcourt Brace Jovanovich, 1977.

Tedesco, N. S. Patterns in prime time. *Journal of Communication*, 1974, *24*, 119–124.

Turow, J. Advising and ordering: Daytime, prime time. *Journal of Communication*, 1974, *24* (2), 138–141.

Ullian, D. Z. The development of conceptions of masculinity and femininity. In B. Lloyd and J. Archer (eds.), *Exploring sex differences*. London: Academic Press, 1976.

U.S. Civil Rights Commission. *Window dressing on the set: Women and minorities in television*. Washington, D.C.: Government Printing Office, 1977.

Verna, M. E. The female image in children's TV commercials. *Journal of Broadcasting*, 1975, *19* (3), 234–242.

Vogal, S., et al. *Sesame Street and sex-role stereotypes (Updated with suggestions for eliminating objectionable features)*. Pittsburgh: Know, Inc., 1973.

Weitzman, L. J., et al. Sex-role socialization in picture books for pre-school children. *American Journal of Sociology,* 1970, *77,* 1125–1150.

Welch, R. L., Huston-Stein, A., Wright, J. C., and Plehal, R. Subtle sex-role cues in children's commercials. *Journal of Communication,* 1979, *29*(3), 202–209.

Williams, F., La Rose, R., and Frost, F. *Children, television, and sex-role stereotyping.* New York: Praeger, 1981.

Williams, J. E., Bennet, S. M., and Best, D. L. Awareness and expression of sex stereotyping in young children. *Developmental Psychology,* 1975, *6,* 635–642.

Women on Words and Images. *Dick and Jane as victims: Sex stereotypes in children's readers.* Princeton, N.J.: Women on Words and Images, 1972.

Women on Words and Images. *Channeling children.* Princeton, N.J.: Women on Words and Images, 1975.

Yorburg, B. *Sexual identity: Sex roles and social change.* New York: Wiley, 1974.

TV AND MINORITIES

Allen, R. L., and Bielby, W. T. Black's attitudes and behaviors toward television. *Communication Research,* 1979, *6*(4), 437–462.

Allen, R. L., and Clarke, D. E. Ethnicity and mass media behavior: A study of Blacks and Latinos, *Journal of Broadcasting,* 1980, *24*(1), 23–33.

Allen, Richard L. Communication research on black Americans. In Howard Myrick (ed.) *In Search of Diversity: Symposium on Minority Audiences and Programming Research.* Washington D.C.: Corporation for Public Broadcasting, Office of Communication Research, 1981.

Ashmore, R. D., and McConahay, J. B. *Psychology and America's urban dilemmas.* New York: McGraw-Hill, 1975.

Atkin, C., Greenberg, B. and McDermott, S. Race and social role learning from television. Paper presented at ACT research workshop, Televised Role Models and Young Adolescents, Harvard Graduate School of Education, November 1977.

Bandura, A. *Principles of behavior modification.* New York: Holt, Rinehart & Winston, 1969.

Baptista-Fernandez, P. and Greenberg, B. S. The context, characteristics, and communication behaviors of blacks on television. In B. Greenberg, (ed.), *Life on television: Content analysis of U.S. TV drama.* Norwood, N.J.: Ablex, 1980.

Barcus, F. E. *Commercial children's television on weekends and weekday afternoons.* Newtonville: Action for Children's Television, 1978a.

Barcus, F. E. Ethical problems in television advertising to children. In B. Rubin (ed.), *Questioning media ethics.* New York: Praeger, 1978b.

Barcus, F. E. *Television in the after-school hours.* Newtonville: Action for Children's Television, 1975a.

Barcus, F. E. (with Wolkin, R.). *Children's television: An analysis of programming and advertising.* New York: Praeger, 1977.

Becker, C.R.S. Language strategies in media content directed to black primary children: A content analysis of selected books, films, and television. *Dissertation Abstract International,* 1974, *36* (3), 1165.

Bogart, L. Negro and white media exposure: New evidence, *Journalism Quarterly,* 1972, *49,* 15–21.

Bower, R. T. *Television and the public.* New York: Holt, Rinehart and Winston, 1973.

Brigham, J. C. Ethnic stereotypes. *Psychological Bulletin,* 1971, *76* (1), 15–38.

Cantor, Muriel G. *Prime-time television: Content and control,* Beverly Hills: Sage Publications, 1980.

Clark, C. Race, identification and television violence. In G. A. Comstock, E. A. Rubinstein, and J. P. Murray (eds.), *Television and social behavior,* Vol. 5, *Television's effects: Further explorations.* Washington, D.C.: Government Printing Office, 1972.

Clark, C. C. Television and social control: Some observations on the portrayal of ethnic minorities. *Television Quarterly,* 1969, *8,* 18-22

Comstock, G., and Cobbey, R. E. Television and the children of ethnic minorities, *Journal of Communication,* 1979, *29* (1), 104–115.

Donagher, P. G., Poulos, R. W., Liebert, R. M., and Davidson, E. S. Race, sex and social example: An analysis of character portrayals on inter-racial television entertainment. *Sociological Reports,* 1975, *37,* 1023–1034.

Donohue, T. R. Black children's perceptions of favorite TV characters as models of antisocial behavior. *Journal of Broadcasting,* 1975, *19* (2), 153–167.

Donohue, T. R. Effect of commercials on black children. *Journal of Broadcasting,* 1975, *15* (6). 41–47.

Eastman, H. A., and Liss, M. B. Ethnicity and children's TV preferences. *Journalism Quarterly,* 1980, 277–280.

Gerbner, G. Violence in television drama. In G. A. Comstock, and E. A. Rubinstein (eds.), *Television and social behavior,* Vol. 1, *Media content and control.* Washington, D.C.: Government Printing Office, 1972.

Gerbner, G., and Signorielli, N. *Women and minorities in television drama: 1969–1978: Research report.* Annenberg School of Communications, Philadelphia, in collaboration with the Seven Actors Guild, AFL-CIO, October 29, 1979.

Greenberg, B. S. Children's reactions to TV blacks. *Journalism Quarterly,* 1972, *49,* 5-14.

Greenberg, B. S. *Life on television: Content analysis of U.S. TV drama.* Norwood, N.J.: Ablex, 1980.

Greenberg, B. S., and Atkin, C. K. Learning about minorities from television. Paper presented at the Annual Meeting of the Association for Education in Journalism, Seattle, August, 1978.

Greenberg, B.S., and Baptista-Fernandez, P. Hispanic Americans: The new minority on television. In B. Greenberg, (ed.), *Life on television: Content analysis of U.S. TV drama.* Norwood, N.J.: Ablex, 1980.

Hartman, P., and Husband, C. *Racism and the mass media.* London: Davis-Paynter, 1974.

Hinton, J. L., Seggar, J. F., Northcott, H. C., and Fontes, B. F. Tokenism and improving the imagery of blacks in TV drama and comedy: 1973. *Journal of Broadcasting,* 1974, *18* (4), 423–432.

Jeffries, L. W., and Hur, K. White ethnics and their media images. *Journal of Communication,* 1979, *29* (1), 116–122.

Jones, S. C. Self and interpersonal evaluations: Esteem theories versus consistency theories. *Psychological Bulletin,* 1973, *79,* 185–199.

Klineberg, O. The scientific study of national stereotypes. *International Social Science Bulletin,* 1951, *3,* 505–515.

Lyle, J., and Hoffman, H. Children's use of television and other media. In E. Z. Rubinstein, G. A. Comstock, and J. P. Murray (eds.), *Television and social behavior,* Vol. 4, *Television in day-to-day life: Patterns of use.* Washington, D.C.: Government Printing Office, 1972.

Mendelson, G., and Young, M. Network children's programming: A content analysis of black and minority treatment on children's television. Paper presented for Black Efforts for Soul in Television, in cooperation with Action for Children's Television, Washington, D.C., August 1972.

Meyer, T. P. Children's perceptions of their favorite TV characters as behavioral models. *Educational Broadcasting Review,* 1973, *7,* 18–33.

Mischel, W. A social-learning view of sex difference. In E. Maccoby (ed.), *The development of sex differences.* Stanford: Stanford University Press, 1966.

Morris, N. S. *Television's child.* Boston: Little, Brown, 1971.

Murray, J. P. *Television and youth: 25 years of research and controversy.* Boys Town, Nb.: Boys Town Press, 1980.

Noble, G. *Children in front of the small screen.* Beverly Hills: Sage Publications, 1975.

Reid, P. T. Racial stereotyping on television. *Journal of Applied Psychology,* 1979, *64* (5), 465–471.

Roberts, C. The portrayal of blacks on network television. *Journal of Broadcasting,* 1970–71, *15* (1), 45–53.

Seggar, J. F., and Wheeler, P. World of work on TV: Ethnic and sex representation in TV drama. *Journal of Broadcasting,* 1973, *17* (2), 201–214.

Seggar, J. F., Hafen, J. K., and Hannonen-Gladden, H. Television's portrayals of minorities and women in drama and comedy drama 1971–1980. *Journal of Broadcasting,* 1981, *25* (3), 277–288.

Signorielli, N. Content analysis: More than just counting minorities. In H. Myrick (ed.) *In search of diversity: Symposium on minority audiences and programming research.* Washington, D.C.: Corporation for Public Broadcasting, 1981.

Tedesco, N. S. Patterns in prime time. *Journal of Communication,* 1974, *24,* 119–124.

Television and social behavior: A technical report submitted to the U.S. Surgeon General's Scientific Advisory Committee. Washington, D.C.: Government Printing Office, 1972.

U.S. Civil Rights Commission. *Window dressing on the set: Women and minorities in television.* Washington, D.C.: Government Printing Office, 1977.

Ward, S. Children's reactions to commercials. *Journal of Advertising Research,* 1972, *14* (3), 37–43.

TV AND THE FAMILY

Allen, W. R. The search for applicable theories of black family life. *Journal of Marriage and the Family.* February 1978, 117–129.

Barcus, F. E. *Commercial Children's Television on Weekends and Weekday Afternoons: A Content Analysis of Children's Programming and Advertising Broadcast in October 1977.* Newtonville: Action for Children's Television, 1978.

Barcus, F. E. Parental influence on children's television viewing. *Television Quarterly,* 1969, *8* (3), 63–73.

Barcus, F. E. and Wolkin, R. *Children's Television: An Analysis of Programming and Advertising.* New York: Praeger, 1977.

Benson, L. *The Family Bond.* New York: Random House, 1971.

Blood, Jr., R. O. Social class and family control of television viewing. *Merrill-Palmer Quarterly of Behavior and Development.* 1961, *7* (3), 205–222.

Boston Globe. October 28, 1981, p. 53.

Bauer, C. F. A descriptive study of selected children's books and television programs as supplements to family life education. *Dissertation,* University of Oregon, 1971.

Brody, G. H., Z. Stoneman, and A. Sanders. Effects of television viewing on family interactions: an observational study. *Family Relations,* 1980, *29,* 216–220.

Busby, L. J. Sex-role research on the mass media. *Journal of Communication,* 1975, *25* (4), 107–131.

Chaffee, S. H., and McCleod, J. M. Adolescent television use in the family context. In G. A. Comstock and E. A. Rubinstein (eds.). *Television and Social Behavior.* Vol. 3: *Television and Adolescent Aggressiveness.* Washington, D.C.: Government Printing Office, 1972, pp. 149–172.

Clavan, S. The family process: a sociological model. *The Family Coordinator,* October 1969, 312–317.

Comstock, George. The effects of television on children and adolescents: the evidence so far. *Journal of Communication,* Autumn 1975, 25–34.

Crano, W. D. and Aronoff, J. A cross-cultural study of expressive and instrumental role complementarity in the family. *American Sociological Review,* 1978, *43,* 463–471.

Dunham, R. M. *Final Report of the Conference on the Family as a Unit of Study in Social Problems*, Vol. 1. Washington, D.C.: Department of Health, Education and Welfare, December 1970.

Eshelman, J. R. *The Family: An Introduction*. Boston: Allyn and Bacon, 1974.

Eversoll, D. A two generational view of fathering. *The Family Coordinator*, 1979, *28* (4), 503–508.

Fisher, C. D. Marital and familial roles on television: an explanatory sociological analysis. *Dissertation Abstracts International*, 1974, p. 599A.

Foster, J. E. Father images: television and ideal. *Journal of Marriage and the Family*, August 1964, 353–355.

Gerbner, G. Violence in television drama: trends and symbolic functions. In G. A. Comstock and E. A. Rubinstein (eds.). *Television and Social Behavior*, Vol. 1: *Media Content and Control*. Washington, D.C.: Government Printing Office, 1972.

Greenberg, B., and Neuendorf, K. Black family interactions on television. In *Life on Television: Content Analyses of U.S. TV Drama*. Norwood, N.J.; Ablex, 1980, pp. 173–181.

Greenberg, B., Buerkel-Rothfuss, N., Neudendorf, K. and Atkin, C. Three seasons of television family role interactions. In *Life on Television: Content Analysis of U.S. TV Drama*. Norwood, N.J.: Ablex, 1980, pp. 161–172.

Greenberg, B., Hines, M., Buerkel-Rothfuss, N., and Atkin, C. Family role structures and interactions on commercial television. In *Life on Television: Content Analysis of U.S. TV Drama*. Norwood, N.J.: Ablex, 1980, pp. 149–160.

Homberg, E. Children and Parents in our television programmes. *Programme of the Prix Jeunesse Seminar 1977*. Washington, D.C.: Department of Health, Education and Welfare, June 1977.

Journal of Communication. Women: nine reports on role, image, and message. *Journal of Communication*, Spring 1974, *24* (2), 103–156.

Klineberg, O., and Klapper, J. T. *The Mass Media: Their Impact on Children and Family Life*. New York: Television Information Office, 1960.

Knox, D. Trends in marriage and the family—the 1980's. *Family Relations*, 1980, *29* (2), 145–150.

Leo, J. New frontier for feminism: Friedan says the family needs attention. *Time*, October 12, 1981, p. 118.

Lewis, R. A. and Pleck, J. Men's roles in the family. *The Family Coordinator,* 1979, *28* (4), 429–432.

Lewis, J. M., and McMillen, D. A Study of Black and White Family Attitudes Toward Television Usage and Competing Activities. Paper presented at Conference on Popular Culture, Toledo, Ohio, April, 1972.

Long, M. L. and Simon, R. The roles and statuses of women on children's and family programs. *Journalism Quarterly,* 1974, *51,* 107–110.

McDonagh, E. C. Television and the family. *Sociology and Social Research,* 1950, *35* (2), 113–121.

McLeod, J. M., Atkin, C., and Chaffee, S. Adolescents, parents, and television use: adolescent self-report measures from Maryland and Wisconsin samples. In G. A. Comstock and E. A. Rubinstein (eds.), *Television and Social Behavior* Vol. 3: *Television and Adolescent Aggressiveness.* Washington, D.C.: U.S. Government Printing Office, 1972, pp. 173–238.

Meyer, Timothy P. Children's perception of favorite television characters as behavioral models. *Educational Broadcasting Review,* 7 (1), February 1973, 25–33.

Miller, W. C., and Beck, T. How do TV parents compare to real parents? *Journalism Quarterly,* 1976, 325–328.

Newcomb, A. F., and Collins, W. A. Children's comprehension of family role portrayals in televised dramas: Effects of socioeconomic status, ethnicity, and age. *Developmental Psychology,* 1979, *15* (4), 417–423.

Petrich, B., and Chadderdon, H. Family beliefs of junior high school pupils. *The Family Coordinator,* October 1969, 374–378.

Reiss, I. L. *The Family System in America.* New York: Holt, Rinehart & Winston, 1979.

Seward, R. R. *The American Family.* Beverly Hills and London: Sage Publications, 1978.

Singer, J., and Singer, D. Television; a member of the family. *National Elementary School Principal,* 1977, *56,* 50–53.

Stencel, S. *The Changing American Family.* Washington, D.C.: Congressional Quarterly, 1979.

Stein, P. J., Richman, J. and Hannon, N. *The Family: Functions, Conflicts, and Symbols.* Reading, Mass.: Addison-Wesley, 1977.

Tognoli, J. The flight from domestic space: men's roles in the household. *The Family Coordinator,* 1979, *28* (4), 599–607.

Wakefield, R. A., Allen, C., and Washchuck, G. *Family Research: A Source Book, Analysis, and Guide to Federal Funding.* Vols. 1 and 2. Westport, Conn.: Greenwood Press, 1979.

Waters, H. F. The TV Fun house. *Newsweek,* May 15, 1979.

Winick, M., and Winick, C. *The Television Experience: What Children See.* Beverly Hills: Sage Publications, 1979.

Author Index

Subject Index

About the Author

Since obtaining his doctorate in communication at the University of Illinois, F. EARLE BARCUS has spent three decades in the analysis of mass media content and its effects on viewers. Presently he is Director of the Communication Research Center, Boston University, School of Public Communication where he is studying various aspects of children's television. He has published many original studies and is the author of CHILDREN'S TELEVISION: AN ANALYSIS OF PROGRAMMING AND ADVERTISING, Praeger.